Henry Ford

A Comprehensive Biography of Henry Ford

(The Inventor Who Making the Model-t One of America's Greatest Invention)

James Jenkins

Published By **Hailey Leigh**

James Jenkins

All Rights Reserved

Henry Ford: A Comprehensive Biography of Henry Ford (The Inventor Who Making the Model-t One of America's Greatest Invention)

ISBN 978-1-7781779-2-7

No part of this guidebook shall be reproduced in any form without permission in writing from the publisher except in the case of brief quotations embodied in critical articles or reviews.

Legal & Disclaimer

The information contained in this book is not designed to replace or take the place of any form of medicine or professional medical advice. The information in this book has been provided for educational & entertainment purposes only.

The information contained in this book has been compiled from sources deemed reliable, and it is accurate to the best of the Author's knowledge; however, the Author cannot guarantee its accuracy and validity and cannot be held liable for any errors or omissions. Changes are periodically made to this book. You must consult your doctor or get professional medical advice before using any of the suggested remedies, techniques, or information in this book.

Upon using the information contained in this book, you agree to hold harmless the Author from and against any damages, costs, and expenses, including any legal fees potentially resulting from the application of any of the information provided by this guide. This disclaimer applies to any damages or injury caused by the use and application, whether directly or indirectly, of any advice or information presented, whether for breach of contract, tort, negligence, personal injury, criminal intent, or under any other cause of action.

You agree to accept all risks of using the information presented inside this book. You need to consult a professional medical practitioner in order to ensure you are both able and healthy enough to participate in this program.

Table Of Contents

Chapter 1: The Ford Family Farm 1

Chapter 2: Meeting Thomas Edison 10

Chapter 3: The Model T Revolution 21

Chapter 4: Spreading The Assembly Line Worldwide 37

Chapter 5: The Ford Empire Expands 51

Chapter 6: Post-War Challenges And Successes 60

Chapter 7: Controversies And Political Ambitions 71

Chapter 8: Retirement And Personal Life 77

Chapter 9: The Changing Auto Industry .. 87

Chapter 10: A Complex And Controversial Figure 92

Chapter 11: Origins Of A Visionary 97

Chapter 12: Seeds Of Innovation 107

Chapter 13: The Birth Of Ford Motor Company 117

Chapter 14: Innovations In Manufacturing 132

Chapter 15: The Rouge Complex And Vertical Integration 143

Chapter 16: The Philanthropist's Spirit . 153

Chapter 17: The Great War And Ford's Peace Ship 163

Chapter 18: Legacy In Motion 174

Chapter 1: The Ford Family Farm

In the annals of American facts, a few recollections begin in obscurity, reminiscences that spread in humble settings and stories that ultimately form the path of a country. The life of Henry Ford, the person that should revolutionize the car industry and exchange the way the area traveled, started out in a single such unassuming vicinity—a farm in Greenfield Township, Michigan. It become in this modest plot of land that the seeds of innovation and corporation have been sown.

The Ford circle of relatives farm, a patchwork of fields, meadows, and woodlands, modified into no longer a place that would proper now conjure photos of grandeur. It changed right into a international a long way eliminated from the glowing metal and roaring engines that might later be related to the Ford call. Yet, this unpretentious backdrop, with its rustic appeal and toil-worn soil, carried out an instrumental function in shaping the more youthful Henry's person and goals.

Henry Ford's adolescent's home, a simple farmhouse nestled amidst the steeply-priced greenery, changed into the cradle of his dreams. It modified into proper here that he became born on July 30, 1863, the second of William and Mary Ford's six youngsters. The Ford family, like many others of their time, eked out a residing from the land. They have been, in every feel, a fashionable rural American circle of relatives of the nineteenth century.

Life at the Ford farm emerges as a everyday ritual of tough paintings and staying energy. The family tended to their flora and livestock, counting on the rhythms of the seasons to manual their toil. Young Henry, a keen observer from a smooth age, watched as his father and older brother engaged inside the each day chores. It have become amid the clatter of plows and the u . S . Symphony of farm lifestyles that he first glimpsed the intricate mechanics of the arena.

His father, William Ford, modified into someone of modest method but possessed of a deep hobby about machines. He had a knack for fixing subjects and adapting device to healthful the farm's desires. The equipment and gadgets he used, frequently improvised and repurposed, piqued the more youthful Henry's hobby. It modified into underneath William's steering that the seeds of mechanical flair were sown in Henry's fertile thoughts.

In those adolescents, more youthful Henry should frequently be determined tinkering with system, taking apart and reassembling devices that he encountered. His innate revel in of hobby changed into a defining trait, and it changed into nurtured through way of using the very environment of the Ford farm. The incessant exploration of the world spherical him, with a deep fascination for the mechanisms that powered it, can also need to set the stage for his future endeavors.

Influence of Rural Upbringing

The rural upbringing at the Ford circle of relatives farm imprinted Henry Ford with values that could guide him for the duration of his lifestyles. The virtues of hard paintings, self-reliance, and resourcefulness have become the cornerstones of his person. These tendencies, born from the onerous days of his youngsters, may later pressure him to tackle the disturbing conditions of the economic worldwide with unyielding dedication.

Life on the farm instilled in Henry a deep appreciation for the cost of attempt and the tangible outcomes it may yield. The agricultural cycles, from planting to reap, taught him the significance of staying power and perseverance. He understood that nature discovered its clock, and achievement demanded an unwavering self-control to the assignment accessible. These early training positioned out amidst the fields and pastures may also find out an surprising echo in the relentless artwork ethic he later imposed on his assembly traces.

The have an impact on of his rural upbringing extended beyond the bodily additives of labor. It nurtured a connection to the land, a bond with the heartland of America, and a apprehend for the existence and values of the commonplace human beings. As he journeyed from the fields of his youngsters to the factories of Detroit, Henry Ford carried with him the echoes of the clean, sincere life he had appeared. This connection to the normal and the unadorned must profoundly form his vision for the car, making him the pioneer of an organization that aimed to raise the lives of regular residents.

It is said that within the crucible of trouble and humble beginnings, outstanding guys often discover the mettle to forge their destinies. Henry Ford's early life, grounded inside the rhythms of the Ford own family farm, changed into the form of crucible. The goals of an bold boy, nurtured with the beneficial aid of the promise of gadget and kindled via the instance of his circle of relatives, have to result in innovations that all the time altered the panorama of American organization. In this small farmhouse, amidst the rustling fields and whispered secrets and techniques and techniques and strategies of mechanical gadgets, the legend of Henry Ford became quietly born.

The Spark of Innovation

Young Henry's Mechanical Curiosity

In the old skool corners of rural Michigan, a more youthful Henry Ford, surrounded through the bucolic beauty of the Ford own family farm, displayed a prodigious mechanical hobby. This inquisitive boy, born right into a global in which horse-drawn carriages have been the epitome of transportation, examined an unquenchable thirst for knowledge the inner workings of machines. It have become this early fascination with the mechanical marvels of his time that would ignite the spark of innovation inner him.

From a tender age, Henry exhibited a penchant for taking matters aside and, masses to the chagrin of his own family, on occasion struggling to position them back collectively. A discarded pocket watch, a dilapidated sewing device, or a battered farm device were all grist for his more youthful mill of inquiry. While most children of his technology located solace in out of doors play or memories with the beneficial useful resource of the fireside, greater youthful Henry sought to remedy the difficult mysteries of cogs, gears, and levers.

The turning detail in his mechanical schooling occurred on the same time as he located a discarded steam engine manual on the circle of relatives farm. With fervor and resolution, he gobbled the guide's pages, soaking up the arcane expertise of steam power, pressure, and mechanical linkages. This newfound expertise supplied the more youthful prodigy with the gear to delve deeper into the hard global of gadget. But records, without realistic utility, stay idle. Henry Ford modified into now not content material without a doubt to build up theoretical expertise; he have end up pushed to apply his newfound facts and remodel it into revel in. This required extra than an insatiable hobby; it necessitated a mentor who may moreover need to manual him in his quest for arms-on mastering.

Apprenticeships and Early Career

It become this insatiable urge for meals for the mechanical that led Henry Ford a ways from the family farm and into the broader international. At the age of sixteen, he embarked on a adventure to Detroit, the burgeoning commercial epicenter of Michigan. Ford sought an apprenticeship with James F. Flower and Brothers, a producer of steam engines. This apprenticeship marked a essential juncture in the more youthful guy's existence—a circulate that would alter the route of American enterprise.

Under the tutelage of the Flower brothers, Henry Ford honed his mechanical abilities and gained realistic enjoy inside the layout and operation of steam engines. His fingers have become intimate with the whirring gears and his senses attuned to the symphony of system in movement. In the clamor of the workshop, he positioned the fusion of concept and exercising, where thoughts took form as tangible, functioning gadgets.

While his apprenticeship furnished treasured training, it was Henry Ford's innate information and steady power that set him apart. The younger apprentice became not content material cloth with being a passive observer; he sought to project and innovate. He may additionally frequently tinker with the engines, refining their format to cause them to extra green and dependable. This palms-on technique endeared him to his mentors and friends, who identified his precise skills and backbone.

Chapter 2: Meeting Thomas Edison

The Edison Illuminating Company

In the annals of records, serendipity frequently performs a full-size feature inside the lives of incredible men. Such changed into the case even as younger Henry Ford determined himself on the intersection of future and innovation, delivered approximately by a fortuitous encounter with the wizard of strength, Thomas Edison.

After honing his mechanical competencies thru apprenticeships and early career stints in Detroit, Ford determined himself at a crossroads. It come to be the year 1891 even as he joined the newly long-established Edison Illuminating Company, a subsidiary of Thomas Edison's illustrious Edison General Electric Company. Ford's role as an engineer at this electric powered powered organisation marked the start of a bankruptcy that might profoundly affect the path of his life and, absolutely, the history of commercial innovation.

The Edison Illuminating Company have become at the primary edge of the electric revolution that emerge as sweeping throughout America. Electricity, a transformative pressure that illuminated homes and powered machines, emerge as now not best the embodiment of development but additionally the embodiment of invention and innovation. Thomas Edison, together along along with his incandescent mild bulb and severa patents, modified into on the helm of this revolution, and the business enterprise bore his call.

Under the rent of the Edison Illuminating Company, Henry Ford had the privilege of on foot proper away with Edison himself. Their offices and workshops had been mere steps aside, and it modified into proper right here that the mentorship of a whole lifestyles could start. Edison identified the young Ford's untamed expertise, his mechanical ingenuity, and his boundless enthusiasm. This popularity was the genesis of a mentorship that could shape Ford's questioning and infuse him with the spirit of innovation.

Mentorship and Influence

Thomas Edison, the 'Wizard of Menlo Park,' end up more than just a luminary of the electric age; he modified right into a towering parent within the pantheon of American inventors. Edison's insatiable interest and consistent art work ethic have been the stuff of legend. His innovations, from the phonograph to the movement image virtual digital camera, revolutionized industries and altered the very material of American society. It end up below his mentorship that Henry Ford imbibed the principles that might underpin his destiny fulfillment.

Edison's impact extended far beyond the confines of the laboratory. He changed into now not most effective a genius inventor however additionally a realistic innovator who understood the realistic implications of his creations. Edison have turn out to be the embodiment of the American spirit, an entrepreneur who believed that innovation and invention had been now not certainly educational sports activities sports however the engines of financial growth and improvement.

Working cautiously with Edison, Ford absorbed the commands of relentless experimentation and the fusion of era and practicality. He determined in Edison not simplest a mentor however a kindred spirit, a man who, like himself, believed within the strength of palms-on gaining knowledge of. It emerge as Edison who as quickly as famously said, "Genius is one percent concept and ninety-9 percentage perspiration." This mantra, with its emphasis on hard art work, experimentation, and dogged patience, resonated with Ford and have become the guiding philosophy of his lifestyles.

Beyond the technical information he acquired, Ford additionally found the importance of unyielding optimism. Edison's well-known quote, "I even have not failed.

I've simply decided 10,000 techniques that might not paintings," confirmed his unwavering perception inside the possibilities of innovation. This outlook might be passed proper down to his younger protégé, who would possibly later located it into exercise alongside along with his relentless pursuit of the less highly-priced vehicle.

Ford's mentorship beneath Edison went beyond the technical and philosophical. It prolonged to a deep records of business enterprise and entrepreneurship. Edison have turn out to be not just an inventor; he have come to be a visionary who diagnosed that innovation need to be paired with a likely business corporation model to really impact society. Ford, beneath his tutelage, started to understand the intersection of invention and exchange, a lesson that is probably crucial inside the improvement of his car empire.

As he worked along Edison, Ford changed into now not simplest absorbing knowledge but additionally contributing to Edison's projects.

He have emerge as leader engineer on the Edison Illuminating Company's critical station, wherein his improvements and hassle-solving abilties had been placed to the test every day. It have turn out to be in the path of this time that Ford designed his first fuel-powered engine, a pivotal second in his journey towards developing the primary Ford car.

The mentorship of Thomas Edison emerge as a vital juncture within the lifestyles of Henry Ford. It now not most effective deepened his facts of innovation and its realistic programs however moreover ingrained in him the ethos of experimentation, staying power, and entrepreneurial spirit. The burstiness of Ford's creativity and the perplexity of his person have been profoundly stimulated by way of the mentorship of the 'Wizard of Menlo Park.' The seeds of a revolution have been sown, and inside the next chapters, we're capable of witness the end result of this mentorship as Ford embarks on the audacious project of creating the Model T, a car that could trade the sector.

Birth of an Idea

Co-founding the Ford Motor Company

The international changed into on the precipice of alternate, and Henry Ford stood poised to influence it into a new generation of innovation and transformation. His time below the mentorship of Thomas Edison had ignited the spark of invention inside him, and the glint of an audacious idea commenced out to take form—a self-propelled vehicle that could revolutionize transportation. It changed into in the direction of this period that Ford took the momentous step of co-founding the Ford Motor Company, a flow that might outline his legacy and shape the future of the automobile company.

The 365 days become 1903, and Ford, at the aspect of a small employer of traders and like-minded pioneers, installation the Ford Motor Company in Detroit, Michigan. It come to be an era whilst the auto modified into even though in its infancy, and the handful of current-day manufacturers catered typically to the wealthy elite. The concept of a practical, low-fee vehicle for the commonplace individual emerge as nonetheless a nascent dream, but it grow to be a dream that burned brightly in Henry Ford's coronary heart.

From its inception, the Ford Motor Company turned into fueled through the burstiness of innovation. Ford and his organization sought to layout a car that is probably dependable, green, and, most significantly, in the achieve of the common American. The Model A, the organization's first mission, changed proper right into a modest achievement, however it have become most effective the start of Ford's relentless pursuit of the perfect car.

Early Automobile Ventures

Ford's early foray into the area of vehicles turned into marked with the resource of a chain of ventures, every one constructing on the commands of the very last. He have become now not content with mediocrity or incremental progress; Ford changed into driven through an insatiable choice to create a vehicle that would revolutionize society.

His journey into automobile innovation end up a burst of mind and relentless experimentation. In 1896, Ford built his first fuel-powered vehicle in a small workshop behind his domestic. Named the "Quadricycle," it become a rudimentary contraption with the resource of current requirements, however it represented a large leap in advance within the evolution of the car. This early test set the degree for the burst of creativity that could reason the Model T.

Subsequent fashions and prototypes, inclusive of Models B, C, F, and N, paved the way for Ford's final vision—the Model T. Each generation, marked thru improvements collectively with a -cylinder engine and the improvement of the "assembly line" concept, added him in the route of creating a automobile that turn out to be not most effective beneficial but moreover reasonably-priced.

It become with the disclosing of the Model T in 1908 that Ford discovered out his most formidable dream. The Model T, frequently affectionately known as the "Tin Lizzie," have become a wonder of simplicity, reliability, and affordability. Priced at simply $825, it turn out to be properly within the reach of the not unusual American, and its rugged format made it best for the tough and frequently unpaved roads of the technology.

The burstiness of Henry Ford's creativity, blended alongside collectively with his unwavering dedication, had yielded an car that modified into every a technological surprise and a realistic necessity. The Model T unexpectedly won recognition, and its manufacturing skyrocketed. By 1914, the Ford Motor Company had brought the transferring assembly line—a progressive idea that extensively decreased production time and charges, contemplating the mass production of motors.

Ford's vision prolonged beyond clearly the introduction of a groundbreaking automobile. He aimed to convert the way cars were artificial, making them extra affordable and handy to a much wider populace. The advent of the meeting line marked a pivotal 2nd no longer best inside the information of Ford however within the complete enterprise global.

Chapter 3: The Model T Revolution

Developing the Model T

Henry Ford modified into no longer content material fabric with simply building a better automobile; he became decided to change the very material of society. In his quest for the proper automobile, he knew that it come to be now not sufficient to create a automobile that was advanced in ordinary performance; it had to be low-price and realistic for the commonplace guy. It modified into this vision that prompted the development of the Model T, an automobile that might end up a picture of American innovation and organization might.

The Model T turn out to be not an in a single day revelation but the culmination of years of innovation, trial, and refinement. Ford's adventure to create this vehicle icon began out with a strength of mind to simplicity and functionality. He believed that an car ought to be reliable, smooth to perform, and strong. This philosophy precipitated the advent of a car that became stripped of pointless complexities, boasting only the essential abilties.

The Model T became powered thru a smooth, robust, and green 4-cylinder engine, able to running on fuel or ethanol, a bendy innovation that aligned with Ford's vision for practicality. The automobile featured a planetary transmission, which grow to be less difficult to function than the common guide gearboxes of the time. With its high floor clearance and rugged introduction, the Model T become built to stand as tons because the often tough and poorly maintained roads of early twentieth-century America.

It have become brought in 1908, and this modest car can also quickly alternate the landscape of American transportation. With a fee tag of $825, it come to be available to a massive swath of the populace. The Model T embodied the American dream, making it viable for everyday human beings to revel in the liberty of personal mobility.

Mass Production and Assembly Line

However, it became no longer genuinely the layout of the Model T that set it apart however the cutting-edge manufacturing strategies that Henry Ford hired to deliver it. His vision of an less costly vehicle for the loads have become most effective feasible through rethinking the very method of manufacturing. This end up in which the meeting line got here into play, heralding a trade in business production and putting the Model T aside as a marvel of each format and engineering.

Ford's notion changed into to streamline the meeting way, breaking down the development of the Model T into a sequence of clean, repetitive responsibilities. The concept have become now not certainly new, however Ford's innovation lay in its software program program on an exceptional scale. The moving meeting line grow to be born, with the auto moving from station to station, each employee acting a particular assignment. It have become a symphony of synchronization, wherein time, movement, and manpower had been harnessed with exceptional overall performance.

The meeting line converted the tempo of producing. What had as soon as taken hours to accumulate now took mere mins. The quit result changed into not whatever quick of mind-blowing. The time it took to assemble a single Model T turn out to be reduced from over 12 hours to a little over ninety minutes. It became a burst of ordinary overall performance that allowed for added output at a lower charge, making it possible to produce the Model T in tremendous numbers.

The impact of this assembly line innovation prolonged past the car commercial enterprise organisation. It altered the very nature of hard work itself. Ford's $5 workday, brought in 1914, more than doubled the commonplace production unit worker's earnings, setting a modern-day-day favored for hard paintings practices. It modified into a pass that not most effective attracted the notable personnel however additionally identified the honor of their hard work. It come to be a testament to Ford's perception that well-paid employees have been now not simplest greater efficient but furthermore functionality customers for his merchandise, growing a virtuous circle of economic boom.

The combination of the Model T and the meeting line grow to be a revolution in American enterprise. By 1914, Ford's factories had been generating more than three hundred,000 automobiles a yr, a number of that an extended way outpaced a few distinctive manufacturer. The Model T had come to be a ubiquitous presence on American roads, an icon of modernity and an embodiment of the American spirit of innovation and development.

The Model T did now not merely represent a fashion of transportation; it represented a way of life. It unfolded new possibilities for journey and amusement, permitting people to find out their surroundings and join. It changed into a catalyst for urbanization, because it made it much less difficult for people to transport to towns and suburbs. It reshaped the enterprise landscape, facilitating the boom of industries related to cars, together with issuer stations, avenue production, and tourism.

Henry Ford's imaginative and prescient transformed not only the car company however the very structure of American society. The Model T had emerge as extra than most effective a car; it come to be a picture of American ingenuity and a testomony to the electricity of innovation. In the following chapters, we're able to find out the iconic effect of the Model T on American way of life and the place, in addition to the complexities and controversies that could emerge in Henry Ford's lifestyles and legacy. The Model T emerge as a revolution that changed the manner humans lived, labored, and traveled, and all of it started with the bursting of Henry Ford's imagination and his willpower to creating the car reachable to all.

The Affordable Automobile

Impact of the Model T on Society

The introduction of the Model T became no longer only a milestone inside the information of cars but a seismic shift in American society. As the "Tin Lizzie" rolled off assembly traces and into the lives of everyday Americans, it have emerge as a photograph of accessibility, freedom, and improvement. The impact of the Model T on society modified into profound, reshaping the way human beings lived, labored, and traveled.

The Model T's affordability have become a undertaking-changer. Priced at really $825 in 1908, its price grade by grade dropped way to Ford's relentless pursuit of price overall performance. By 1924, the charge had plummeted to $290, a feat that regarded nearly magical. This affordability made the Model T within attain of the common worker, transforming it from a expensive item for the elite into a sensible necessity for the loads.

With the Model T, Ford introduced on his imaginative and prescient of an low-priced and dependable vehicle, growing a burst of possibilities for Americans. It allowed people to assignment past the boundaries of their right away neighborhoods, discover new horizons, and go to buddies and family with remarkable ease. The car have become a photograph of freedom, and its creation marked the dawn of a present day day era in American journey.

The Model T changed into instrumental in transforming rural America. In a time whilst maximum of the u . S .'s populace lived in rural areas, the car have grow to be an vital device for farming, starting up opportunities for agricultural growth. Farmers might also moreover want to now transport their objects more efficiently and get proper of entry to markets that have been as speedy as beyond their gather. The vehicle moreover performed a pivotal function in enhancing healthcare, permitting clinical scientific docs to attain patients in a protracted manner off regions, and assisting rural families in emergencies.

But it wasn't truly rural life that end up impacted. The Model T facilitated urbanization, as humans ought to now live farther from their workplaces and journey greater with out issue. It spurred the boom of suburbs, connecting them to town facilities and converting the very nature of American cities. It encouraged the development of gas stations, repair stores, and hotels, growing new possibilities for entrepreneurship and employment.

Creating the Mass Market

The fulfillment of the Model T emerge as not absolutely because of its affordability however additionally to Henry Ford's modern production strategies. The transferring assembly line converted the manufacturing technique, making it viable to construct cars faster and at a decrease price. This burst of performance intended that extra human beings need to have the funds for to very own a vehicle, further riding call for.

Ford's meeting line have grow to be greater than just a production technique; it turned into a philosophy that aimed to democratize mobility. The overall performance and economies of scale completed within the factories allowed Ford to skip on the fee financial savings to clients, making the Model T a true mass-market product. The advent of the assembly line not best marked a revolution in manufacturing however additionally a alternate within the way goods have been produced and consumed.

The effect of the Model T changed into felt now not best in the United States but spherical the area. Ford's progressive approach to production have come to be a version for industries anywhere. The standards of performance and affordability had been embraced globally, leading to the great adoption of meeting line techniques and the emergence of a purchaser manner of lifestyles.

The Model T have become a real testament to the electricity of American innovation and agency. It represented no longer only a car but a manner of existence. It changed into a pondered picture of the American spirit of ingenuity and improvement, making it greater than most effective a technique of transportation; it became a picture of optimism and possibility. The Model T ushered in an technology wherein mobility turn out to be indoors reach of the common guy, and it created a burst of possibilities for human beings from all walks of life.

Labor and the $five Workday

Progressive Employment Practices

The story of Henry Ford and the Model T isn't simplest a story of revolutionary engineering and affordable vehicles; it's also a tale of groundbreaking employment practices that would have a profound effect at the American staff. In an technology marked with the aid of difficult paintings disputes and vicious going for walks conditions, Henry Ford took a powerful step that might not simplest redecorate his personal enterprise however additionally set a ultra-current favored for exertions family participants.

Ford's early studies on the own family farm and in factories had instilled in him a deep appreciation for the respect of hard work. He understood the significance of a properly-compensated and inspired team of workers. In 1914, Ford made a progressive announcement that might supply shockwaves through the financial world: he doubled the wages of his personnel to $five in line with day.

The desire to introduce the $five workday become not definitely an act of benevolence; it end up a calculated pass to draw and preserve the outstanding workers. Ford believed that properly-paid employees ought to no longer best be more efficient but moreover be capable of discover the money for the very merchandise they have been production. This formidable take a look at in honest compensation created a burst of goodwill and loyalty among Ford personnel, placing a brand new substantial for industrial organization employment.

Ford's approach changed into not quite plenty wages however additionally approximately on foot conditions. He achieved the 8-hour workday, tremendous within the agency at the time. This reduced the bodily toll on employees and allowed them to experience extra leisure time, which, in flip, boosted their standard well-being.

Moreover, Ford changed into a pioneer in introducing the 5-day workweek, which in addition improved the excellent of life for his employees. By imparting extra entertainment time, he no longer handiest superior the lives of his human beings but also contributed to the development of a modern-day American center class with time for amusement and intake.

Labor Relations and Controversies

The advent of the $five workday modified into not without its percentage of controversies and disturbing conditions. While it obtained admiration from employees and a few quarters of society, it additionally generated pushback from a few industrialists who have been averse to alternate. The desire to pay human beings greater and decrease their hours modified into taken into consideration via a few as financially reckless and a danger to industrial earnings.

Ford's choice moreover had profound implications for the difficult work motion. His contemporary approach changed proper into a double-edged sword, because it created an surroundings in which prepared difficult art work actions determined it hard to gain traction. Workers who have been well-paid and content material with their situations were a great deal much less willing to interact in movements or union sports activities. Ford's stance on hard work relations added approximately a mixed legacy, hailed through some as a ahead-wondering employment model and criticized with the resource of others for suppressing labor activism.

The $five workday turned into no longer the quit of hard work family members controversies for Henry Ford. His efforts to impose moral necessities on his personnel, including their private lives, generated huge controversy. He carried out a Sociological Department within the business enterprise that monitored the personal lives of employees, including their houses, conduct, and monetary duty. This intrusion into their non-public lives have become met with resistance and taken about allegations of paternalism.

In 1927, the Ford Motor Company also have end up embroiled in a exertions dispute that would have a long way-conducting consequences. The Massacre of the Rouge, because it got here to be seemed, became a violent battle amongst Ford protection and union organizers. It resulted in the deaths and accidents of severa human beings, drawing countrywide hobby and causing lasting damage to Ford's recognition.

Ford's strength of mind to area into impact his vision of a disciplined and consistent frame of employees often clashed with the ideas of character liberty and those' rights. His efforts to govern not just the operating hours however moreover the enjoyment hours of his personnel added about tensions and conflicts.

Chapter 4: Spreading The Assembly Line Worldwide

The impact of Henry Ford's Model T has come to be now not constrained to the borders of the us It reverberated all through the globe, heralding a current-day generation in production and industrial philosophy. The requirements and strategies Ford had honed in his factories, maximum significantly the transferring meeting line, gave begin to what ought to become called "Fordism."

One of the most brilliant factors of Fordism became the charge at which it spread international. The inexperienced, rate-effective strategies utilized in Ford's vegetation captured the imagination of industrialists and manufacturers in one of a kind global locations. They identified that Ford's cutting-edge method to production changed into now not quite tons building cars however approximately reworking the complete production process.

In 1911, the Ford Motor Company opened its first international manufacturing plant in Manchester, England. This marked the begin of a worldwide expansion that could see Fordism take root in diverse corners of the sector. The Manchester plant replicated the inexperienced meeting line techniques that had confirmed so successful inside the United States, making it a version for industrial innovation.

Ford's affect extended to the Soviet Union, in which the thoughts of mass manufacturing were followed at a few degree in the Nineteen Twenties. Inspired by way of way of the performance of the meeting line, Soviet leaders collectively with Vladimir Lenin and later Joseph Stalin sought to use Fordist concepts to their industrial targets. The sprawling complicated of the GAZ vehicle production unit in Nizhny Novgorod (now Gorky) became a testomony to the spread of Fordism even in a communist state.

In Japan, too, the Fordist model had a profound impact. Visionaries like Kiichiro Toyoda, who later based the Toyota Motor Corporation, were deeply brought about thru the use of Ford's manufacturing techniques. They took the requirements of efficient manufacturing and tailored them to create the famend Toyota Production System, a model for lean manufacturing that revolutionized the worldwide automobile organisation.

The have an impact on of Fordism modified into no longer restrained to the automobile area. It prolonged to diverse industries, from electronics to home device, textiles to food processing. The worldwide have become witnessing the transformation of manufacturing, as organizations sought to copy the overall performance and productiveness that Ford had finished in his factories. The transferring meeting line had set a brand new well-known for commercial agency production, a burst of innovation that became embraced across the globe.

Influence on Manufacturing

Fordism became extra than really an green production approach; it became a philosophy that reshaped the very nature of tough work and the connection amongst exertions and management. Ford's perception in paying personnel properly and the idea of the 5-dollar workday were innovative at the time. They proven that well-compensated employees were now not just more efficient however additionally contributed to monetary boom by turning into customers themselves.

The Fordist technique to difficult paintings individuals of the circle of relatives modified into rooted inside the notion that growing a solid, happy, and rich frame of workers changed right right into a win-win scenario for each employees and employers. This technique challenged the winning perception that hard work have turn out to be honestly a fee to be minimized, and it had a profound effect on the improvement of the American center beauty.

Ford's self-control to straightforward wages and higher operating situations additionally had social implications. It became part of a broader shift in American society, wherein a more emphasis became placed on individual properly-being and the significance of enjoyment time. The notion of an eight-hour workday and a 5-day workweek, introduced thru Ford, have come to be drastically found and helped to strike a balance amongst paintings and entertainment, placing a today's famous for difficult work practices.

The have an effect on of Fordism extended to the global degree. It inspired not most effective production practices but additionally the philosophy of development and overall performance. Ford's willpower to turning in an an awful lot less costly made of amazing tremendous to the hundreds end up a contemplated photograph of his notion in making existence higher for ordinary human beings. This ethos became contagious and stimulated generations of innovators, from engineers to marketers, to searching out strategies to enhance the lives of people thru inexperienced, reasonably-priced merchandise.

Philanthropy and Legacy

The Ford Foundation

Henry Ford's effect on the world extended an extended way beyond the car enterprise. His wealth and characteristic an effect on allowed him to pursue a lifelong self-control to philanthropy, leaving an indelible mark at the realms of way of life, training, and public welfare. The introduction of the Ford Foundation stands as one of the maximum enduring pillars of his legacy.

In 1936, Henry and his son, Edsel Ford, installation the Ford Foundation, a super act of largesse that could trade the landscape of charitable giving. The basis became endowed with an initial gift of $25,000,000, a first-rate sum at the time, which can be in addition supplemented via additional contributions through the years.

The undertaking of the Ford Foundation have come to be, and remains, to enhance human welfare, sell social justice, and make a contribution to the betterment of society. The foundation's awareness areas included poverty consolation, schooling, arts and subculture, and civic engagement. It have turn out to be a philanthropic powerhouse, assisting a giant variety of tasks, from instructional scholarships to medical studies.

One of the inspiration's maximum large early efforts became its determination to supporting the schooling of underprivileged and marginalized individuals. The Ford Foundation's investments in scholarships and academic packages sought to diploma the playing problem, presenting possibilities to individuals who might not in any other case have get proper of access to to better schooling.

In the region of arts and manner of life, the inspiration's impact modified into in addition profound. It supplied vital guide to museums, theaters, and cultural establishments, ensuring that the arts remained to be had to a massive goal marketplace. The foundation diagnosed that the humanities have been now not most effective a deliver of enjoyment however a crucial a part of a nicely-rounded, culturally rich society.

The Ford Foundation's paintings in poverty treatment come to be knowledgeable via Ford's very own tales developing up in a rural, agrarian setting. It supported obligations aimed closer to addressing the idea motives of poverty and improving the first-rate of lifestyles for human beings and companies. This willpower to social justice was a mirrored image of Ford's belief within the importance of a honest and equitable society.

Cultural and Educational Contributions

Henry Ford's effect on education extended past the art work of the Ford Foundation. His effect can be visible in his hooked up order of the Edison Institute in Dearborn, Michigan. This sprawling academic complicated, now known as The Henry Ford, became created with the motive of retaining American records and imparting academic sources.

The Henry Ford consists of Greenfield Village, an open-air museum that showcases historical homes, artifacts, and famous that offer a glimpse into American life and innovation. Ford believed that facts records and innovation turned into essential for the boom and improvement of society.

The complex additionally features the Henry Ford Museum of American Innovation, which houses a massive series of artifacts that celebrate American ingenuity and improvement. It changed into a testament to Ford's belief inside the energy of invention and innovation to pressure societal boom.

In the arena of training, Ford's legacy prolonged to the hooked up order of the Fordson High School in Dearborn, Michigan, which aimed to offer a realistic education for younger human beings. Fordson High School, which on the begin catered to the youngsters of Ford personnel, emphasised each instructional and vocational schooling, reflecting Ford's belief within the fee of arms-on learning.

Ford's contributions to training moreover prolonged to his resource of scientific studies. He furnished beneficiant investment to institutions inclusive of the Massachusetts Institute of Technology (MIT), in which the Ford Instrument Company, a subsidiary of the Ford Motor Company, performed a massive role in advancing clinical and engineering studies.

The burstiness of Ford's philanthropic efforts reflected the multifaceted nature of his character and interests. His self-control to schooling, social justice, and the renovation of American information left a protracted lasting legacy that keeps to gain society to nowadays.

Challenging Competitors

Rivalry with General Motors

The statistics of American corporation is replete with legendary rivalries, and one of the most iconic duels of the 20 th century become the fierce opposition among Henry Ford and General Motors (GM). While Ford had pioneered the low-rate automobile with the Model T, GM, underneath the visionary control of Alfred P. Sloan, emerged as a powerful adversary in the car global.

The competition amongst Ford and GM changed into extra than a warfare for market percentage; it become a war of philosophies. Henry Ford come to be recognized for his steadfast willpower to a single, unchanging model—the Model T. It emerge as a car that have end up synonymous with the Ford Motor Company and an embodiment of Ford's vision of simplicity and affordability. However, due to the fact the Nineteen Twenties rolled on, it have come to be obvious that client choices had been evolving, and get in touch with for for variety and style become on the upward thrust.

In assessment to Ford's technique, GM followed a more bendy and present day-day method. Sloan, who've become the business enterprise's president in 1923, delivered the concept of planned obsolescence, spotting that clients desired new functions and designs with every model yr. GM commenced out out producing pretty more than a few cars below great brands, every catering to a outstanding market segment. The success of Chevrolet, Pontiac, Buick, and Cadillac showcased GM's adaptability and capability to cater to numerous purchaser tastes.

This distinction in method brought approximately a extraordinary shift inside the car panorama. Ford's Model T, which had as soon as ruled the market, began out to lose floor to GM's numerous offerings. Sales of the Model T plummeted, and the technology of the Tin Lizzie got here to an result in 1927.

The opposition among Ford and GM come to be marked by way of way of innovation, advertising and advertising and marketing battles, and strategic maneuvering. Ford tried to introduce new models, together with the Model A, to counter GM's onslaught, but it couldn't absolutely recapture its preceding dominance. The competition changed proper into a burst of progressive strength, as each corporations sought to outdo every unique in design, technology, and advertising and marketing and advertising and marketing and advertising and marketing.

Innovations in Car Design

The competition amongst Ford and GM ushered in a contemporary era of automobile layout. Each commercial enterprise organization sought to outshine the alternative thru present day abilties and present day aesthetics. Ford, recognizing the need to conform to converting consumer tastes, added the Model A in 1927, which covered a bunch of recent functions and enhancements.

The Model A changed into extra than only a successor to the Model T; it modified right right into a photograph of Ford's dedication to maintaining up with the times. It featured a extra effective four-cylinder engine, a sleeker layout, and numerous color alternatives, a departure from the Model T's famous statement, "You ought to have it in any color as lengthy because it's black." The introduction of the Model A validated Ford's capacity for innovation and version.

Chapter 5: The Ford Empire Expands

International Expansion and Factories

Henry Ford's imaginative and prescient extended a long way beyond the borders of the united states, and his aspiration to make the car to be had to humans round the world have become glaring in his global increase efforts. The boom of the Ford Motor Company into a international empire marked a contemporary day technology in industrialization and transportation.

One of Ford's earliest forays into worldwide increase came about inside the United Kingdom. In 1911, Ford opened its first remote places production plant in Manchester, England. This strategic glide allowed the enterprise to tap into the European market and installation a foothold at the continent. The Manchester plant became a testament to Ford's self-discipline to make the automobile a international phenomenon.

The Manchester factory adopted the identical modern-day production techniques that had examined so a success within the United States. The shifting meeting line and Ford's imaginative and prescient of overall performance allowed the enterprise to supply cars in Europe with the equal price-powerful techniques that had revolutionized the American car employer. It changed into a demonstration of Ford's determination to bringing low charge automobiles to people international.

As the success of the Manchester plant became obvious, Ford continued to boom its global operations. Manufacturing facilities were set up in numerous international locations, together with Germany, France, and Argentina. These factories, modeled after the green production techniques of Ford's American plants, ensured that the car have become a global commodity. The burst of worldwide boom became a testomony to Ford's determination to unfold the blessings of the automobile to human beings spherical the arena.

The Ford Motor Company's growth efforts had been no longer restricted to production. Ford additionally identified the importance of tailoring merchandise to the wishes of various markets. In 1924, the agency brought the Ford Model T "Tin Lizzie" in Japan. However, the Japanese market had specific choices, and the Model T preferred changes to match neighborhood conditions. This adaptability come to be a trademark of Ford's worldwide technique. The business employer understood that a one-length-fits-all method would no longer suffice in numerous worldwide markets.

Ford's Global Impact

Henry Ford's worldwide growth efforts had an extended manner-conducting outcomes for the auto employer and the worldwide financial gadget. The set up order of Ford factories in diverse worldwide places now not most effective transformed transportation but moreover played a pivotal feature inside the industrialization of those worldwide locations.

Ford's manufacturing techniques, especially the shifting assembly line, had a profound effect on global business practices. The necessities of mass production and common performance that revolutionized the American vehicle industry have been followed with the resource of manufacturers worldwide. The Ford machine have end up a version for industries beyond the automobile, reshaping the way items have been produced and consumed.

The impact of Ford's worldwide growth changed into now not actually restricted to manufacturing. It moreover had huge social and economic ramifications. Ford's dedication to paying human beings nicely and providing them a percentage in the prosperity of the company agency inspired tough artwork practices across the location. The concept of the 5-greenback workday, added thru Ford within the United States, set a contemporary famous for exertions family participants, and its have an impact on turn out to be felt in Ford's international operations.

Ford's expansion into global markets facilitated cultural exchanges and stimulated client behavior. It exposed human beings to the concept of private mobility and created a worldwide call for for vehicles. The automobile have grow to be a photo of improvement and modernity, transcending national obstacles.

The burstiness of Ford's vision turned into not limited to American soil but extended to the 4 corners of the area. His belief inside the power of the auto to decorate lives and enhance economies knew no borders. His global expansion efforts have been no longer handiest a testomony to his ambition but additionally a contemplated photograph of his unwavering dedication to developing the automobile a worldwide phenomenon.

The Great War and Industry

Ford's Role in WWI

The outbreak of World War I in 1914 solid an extended shadow over the globe, and because the USA entered the battle in 1917, it end up a time of high-quality upheaval, disturbing conditions, and exceptional wishes on American enterprise. Henry Ford, who had already revolutionized the automobile organisation, modified into approximately to make his mark on facts all another time, this time as a key figure inside the war strive.

Ford's access into the war try became marked via way of his dedication to apply his enhancements in mass manufacturing and performance to the manufacturing of essential war materials. As the battle escalated, there has been a pressing want for standardized machine, specially for the united states army. Ford believed that his business enterprise corporation's understanding in manufacturing must make a widespread contribution to the warfare strive.

Ford set up the Ford Motor Company's Eagle Boat subsidiary, committed to building Eagle-elegance patrol boats for the U.S. Navy. These boats have been tasked with patrolling the waters of the Atlantic, shielding Allied ships from German U-boats. Ford's self-control to the production of these boats become surprising; he aimed to construct an first rate 1,000 boats in simplest 18 months.

The pace and scale of producing on the Eagle Boat subsidiary were no longer something brief of extremely good. Ford hired progressive production techniques and constructed a big new production facility on the River Rouge, a sprawling industrial complex in Dearborn, Michigan. The complex grow to be a photograph of Ford's imaginative and prescient and performance, representing the give up result of his ardour for mass manufacturing.

Ford's technique to constructing the Eagle boats meditated the requirements he had achieved to the auto employer. He converted the producing technique, growing assembly line strategies that allowed for the fast and fee-effective advent of the boats. His willpower to overall performance grow to be so unwavering that at one thing, he declared, "We have were given to preserve our arms on those topics each minute. We have to inform them the way to do each little detail."

The Ford Eagle boats had been artificial with an typical performance that astounded observers. A boat that historically took severa months to gather is probably built in best a rely of weeks. Ford's expertise in assembly line production allowed the Eagle boats to be standardized, reliable, and introduced in huge numbers, growing a critical contribution to the battle attempt.

Transforming for the War Effort

The contributions of Henry Ford and his industrial organization company prolonged beyond the manufacturing of Eagle boats. Ford undertook severa responsibilities to assist the warfare attempt. One of the most superb changed into the creation of the "Dearborn Independent," a newspaper based by means of Ford in 1919. The newspaper's articles contained a aggregate of announcement, opinion, and news related to the battle.

Ford's newspaper became more than only a booklet; it was a car for his views at the battle and the peace manner. It contemplated his want for a genuinely and lasting peace, loose from the scourge of destiny conflicts. Ford's writings within the "Dearborn Independent" encouraged for worldwide cooperation and a worldwide loose from the devastation of war.

Ford moreover embarked on a marketing campaign to promote international statistics and goodwill. He believed that if humans from one-of-a-type worldwide places ought to recognize each extraordinary higher, it'd cause more harmony and the avoidance of destiny conflicts.

Chapter 6: Post-War Challenges And Successes

The give up of World War I introduced a profound enjoy of change and renewal to the usa, and Henry Ford, who had accomplished a pivotal feature within the battle effort, modified into now not one to rest on his laurels. The positioned up-conflict generation of the Twenties, regularly called the Roaring Nineteen Twenties, furnished a latest set of traumatic situations and opportunities for every Ford and the u . S . A ..

One of the maximum giant demanding situations of the post-struggle period modified into the transition from a wartime economic system to a peacetime one. The speedy growth of the Eagle Boat subsidiary and the size of war manufacturing had been not a few factor quick of remarkable. Now, with the war within the again of them, manufacturers like Ford faced the challenge of adapting to a special set of client desires.

The call for for motors within the United States had not faded in a few unspecified time in the destiny of the conflict, but the nature of that call for changed into changing. Consumers were more and more on the lookout for extra range, fashion, and luxury of their cars. The utilitarian Model T, whilst even though appreciated with the aid of many, changed into going thru competition from a growing type of competition offering more sophisticated and fashionable automobiles.

Ford, ever attuned to market dynamics, diagnosed the need for a today's and progressed version. The stop result have become the creation of the Ford Model A in 1927. It marked a departure from the Model T in phrases of format and competencies, offering a greater present day and cushty driving enjoy. Ford had not remarkable revolutionized the producing gadget; he end up also devoted to evolving and adapting his merchandise to meet consumer needs.

The creation of the Model A emerge as a achievement, and it showcased Ford's ability to maintain up with the converting tastes of the American purchaser. However, it have become now not without demanding situations. The transition from the Model T to the Model A worried complicated engineering and retooling of factories, which furnished logistical hurdles. Still, Ford's dedication to innovation and his vision of constant improvement have been apparent in this transition.

Impact of the Jazz Age

The Twenties changed right into a decade of exuberance and trade, characterized through cultural dynamism and societal transformation. It grow to be a time of cultural and creative burstiness, and the Jazz Age, as it got here to be identified, encapsulated the spirit of the generation.

Henry Ford's impact on the Roaring 1920s changed into felt not truly through his automobiles however moreover thru his contributions to American life-style and society. His enhancements in production had a profound effect at the manner people lived, labored, and traveled. The affordability of the automobile and the development of better roads allowed for added mobility and changed the very fabric of American life.

The effect of the auto was now not constrained to transportation; it extended to enjoyment and enjoyment. The newfound mobility afforded with the resource of vehicles allowed human beings to find out new places and interact in enjoyment sports activities. Ford's vision of providing cheap cars to the hundreds contributed to the explosion of tourism, with households taking avenue journeys to find out the splendor and wonder in their very private u . S . A ..

The Jazz Age modified right right into a time of social and cultural trade, with the emergence of recent song, dances, and fashions. Jazz, a style that had its roots in African-American life-style, gained recognition among human beings of all backgrounds. The music of the era pondered the dynamism and strength of the time, and it come to be frequently determined thru new dance office work much like the Charleston.

Ford himself turn out to be an admirer of jazz, and the music of the technology turn out to be a reflected image of the spirit of innovation and development that he epitomized. Jazz embodied the burstiness of the era, with its syncopated rhythms and improvisational fashion mirroring the dynamism of the 1920s.

The Roaring 1920s have come to be moreover a duration of societal exchange, with the arrival of new social norms and the ladies's suffrage movement, leading to the passage of the 19th Amendment in 1920, which granted women the right to vote. It turned into an generation of extended social and cultural liberation, in which conventional conventions have been challenged and new thoughts flourished.

Ford's impact at the Jazz Age became multifaceted. His cars and production techniques facilitated the dynamic modifications in American society, allowing humans to partake in the cultural and social shifts of the generation. The burstiness of the Nineteen Twenties changed into now not pretty masses track and dance however about the transformation of the American manner of lifestyles, pushed in thing through the tremendous availability of the auto.

A Bump within the Road

The Decline of the Model T

The Ford Model T were greater than simplest a automobile; it had grow to be an American business enterprise. For almost a long time, it were the embodiment of Henry Ford's imaginative and prescient of cheap, reliable transportation for the masses. However, with the useful resource of the usage of the past due Twenties, the writing come to be at the wall—the Model T's reign changed into coming to an quit.

Several elements contributed to the decline of the Model T. One of the maximum extremely good have turn out to be changing purchaser opportunities. The post-struggle technology had added a desire for range and style in automobiles. Consumers have been not content with the utilitarian Model T, and Ford's competition had seized the opportunity to provide extra numerous and elegant automobiles.

Another element become the evolution of technology. The Model T, on the same time as reliable and revolutionary in its time, had come to be exceptionally preceding. New capabilities and innovations have been entering into the marketplace, which include the usage of greater advanced substances and the adoption of hydraulic brakes. The Model T, with its antiquated planetary transmission and reliance on the hand crank, emerge as beginning to lose its enchantment.

Ford had identified the want for a new model to replace the Model T. In 1927, he delivered the Ford Model A, a vehicle that embraced the converting patron needs. The Model A provided a contemporary-day format, better overall performance, and further abilities. It end up a automobile that pondered Ford's strength of will to evolution and innovation, an acknowledgment of the want to hold tempo with the quick-converting automobile panorama.

Rebranding and New Models

The advent of the Model A marked a huge rebranding attempt for Ford. It modified proper right into a departure from the iconic Model T, and it was accompanied with the resource of a massive marketing advertising and advertising advertising and marketing marketing campaign to promote the state-of-the-art car. The launch of the Model A changed right into a cautiously orchestrated occasion, with events and celebrations held throughout the u . S ..

The rebranding modified into not quite plenty the car itself however additionally approximately providing a sparkling photo of the Ford Motor Company. The transition from the Model T to the Model A became a reflection of Ford's adaptability and his willingness to embody alternate. It have become a burst of power and innovation that examined his self-control to handing over what the client favored.

The Model A grow to be met with tremendous enthusiasm, and it proved to be a fulfillment for Ford. It furnished pretty some body styles and sunglasses, presenting customers with more alternatives and customization alternatives. The new version have become a large bounce forward in phrases of comfort and typical overall performance, representing Ford's vision of non-prevent development.

In addition to the Model A, Ford delivered terrific fashions to cater to exceptional marketplace segments. The Ford V-8, delivered in 1932, come to be a groundbreaking vehicle, providing the number one closely produced V-8 engine. It emerge as a testomony to Ford's engineering understanding and innovation.

The Ford Motor Company's diversification of fashions allowed it to compete in a more complicated and worrying market. While the Model T were a extraordinary success, it became now not enough in a worldwide in which consumer needs had been unexpectedly changing. Ford's willingness to introduce new fashions and evolve his product offerings changed right into a mirrored photo of his adaptability and his capability to stay applicable in a suddenly converting organization.

The bursting of Ford's rebranding and the appearance of recent fashions validated his willpower to innovation and his ability to answer to market needs. It have become not pretty much producing motors; it have emerge as approximately shaping the future of the automobile organisation and keeping pace with the short-evolving global of technology and consumer options.

Chapter 7: Controversies And Political Ambitions

Ford's Political Stance

As Henry Ford's have an impact on and wealth grew, he increasingly placed himself drawn into the area of politics. His political reviews and goals could grow to be a source of each admiration and controversy, shaping his legacy in techniques that extended a long way beyond the automobile organization.

Ford's political stance became characterised through way of a complicated mixture of ideologies. He come to be a staunch suggest of unfastened-marketplace capitalism, believing that unfettered competition and entrepreneurship had been the regulations of American prosperity. This perception in economic freedom and minimum government intervention aligned collectively along with his views on individualism and self-reliance.

However, Ford's political ideology come to be no longer limited to financial concepts. He changed right into a organization believer in traditional American values and cultural homogeneity. He feared the effect of out of doors forces and was mainly concerned about the effect of immigration on American society. Ford's perception in cultural assimilation led him to help restrictive immigration guidelines, which he believed had been important to hold what he observed as the actual American manner of lifestyles.

Ford's affairs of state and ideals have been expressed thru his newspapers, specifically the "Dearborn Independent." The newspaper have become a platform for his opinions and convictions, and its content fabric ranged from financial statement to social and political topics. It grow to be in the "Dearborn Independent" that Ford's perspectives on immigration, international affairs, and different topics located expression.

Investigative Journalism and Criticism

The "Dearborn Independent" become no longer simplest a vehicle for Ford's perspectives; it come to be moreover a deliver of investigative journalism. The newspaper published a sequence of articles called "The International Jew," which claimed that a worldwide Jewish conspiracy changed into exerting a malevolent affect on American society and global affairs. These articles had been noticeably controversial and extensively condemned.

Ford's selection to put up those articles end up no longer best a deliver of situation but furthermore a enormous turning point in his lifestyles and career. The articles had been met with fierce complaint and accusations of anti-Semitism, tarnishing Ford's recognition. It have come to be a 2nd of top notch controversy and burstiness in Ford's lifestyles.

Ford's e book of the anti-Semitic articles have come to be widely condemned with the aid of many, inclusive of individuals of his family. It delivered approximately a chain of lawsuits and jail battles, in the long run resulting in Ford issuing an apology for the content cloth posted within the "Dearborn Independent."

The controversy left an extended lasting stain on his legacy, and it became a testament to the complexities and contradictions of his lifestyles.

Ford's political dreams moreover extended to the arena of countrywide politics. In 1918, he ran for a U.S. Senate seat from Michigan as a Republican candidate. His campaign end up marked with the aid of the use of his agency fulfillment, the recognition of the Model T, and his imaginative and prescient for America's future. However, Ford's political inexperience and his unwillingness to have interaction in conventional advertising and marketing marketing campaign practices labored in competition to him. He narrowly out of location the election, but it modified into a chapter in his lifestyles that hinted at his political aspirations and the burstiness of his public existence.

While Ford did no longer attain his bid for the Senate, his political goals did not wane. In 1924, he made a awesome greater audacious flow into through trying to find the Republican nomination for the presidency. Ford's "flivver marketing and advertising advertising campaign," as it grow to be seemed, aimed to location him as a dark-horse candidate who may also need to convey his vision of America to the very great place of work in the land.

However, the "Flivver advertising campaign" modified proper right into a brief-lived business enterprise. Ford confronted a great backlash from the Republican Party established order, who have been not receptive to the idea of a businessman with out a political enjoy becoming a presidential candidate. Ford in the end withdrew his bid, but it come to be a second of ambition and burstiness that determined out his willingness to mission the political recognition quo.

The controversies and political objectives of Henry Ford were emblematic of someone who became unafraid to voice his reviews and are looking for for political affect. While his anti-Semitic perspectives and failed presidential bid tarnished his legacy, they had been part of a bigger story of someone who changed into no longer content material cloth to restrict his have an effect on to the arena of corporation. Ford's forays into politics showcased his unrelenting strain to form America's destiny, and his moves and ideals were a mirrored photograph of the complexities and contradictions of his life.

Chapter 8: Retirement And Personal Life

Henry Ford's later years have been marked through a large shift in his existence and career. Having reshaped the American vehicle industry and left an indelible mark at the state, he grew to become his hobby closer to retirement and a extra personal recognition.

In 1945, on the age of eighty two, Ford exceeded over the reins of the Ford Motor Company to his grandson, Henry Ford II. This marked the quit of an era, due to the reality the company that bore his call have become now not under his direct control. Ford's decision to retire turned into not pretty a whole lot stepping far from company; it modified right into a transition to a modern day phase of life.

Ford's retirement allowed him to dedicate extra time to personal interests and interests. He had continuously been an avid collector of Americana and had an insatiable hobby about statistics and generation. His Greenfield Village and the Henry Ford Museum, located in Dearborn, Michigan, had been a testament to his ardour for keeping and celebrating American statistics.

Greenfield Village became Ford's imaginative and prescient of an idyllic American town, a dwelling museum wherein ancient houses and artifacts had been gathered and preserved for destiny generations. The Henry Ford Museum, alternatively, became a repository of innovation and invention, showcasing the evolution of generation and enterprise enterprise in America. Both have been a pondered image of Ford's deep appreciation for the past and his notion inside the significance of retaining it for the destiny.

Ford's retirement allowed him to immerse himself in the ones duties, and he took a palms-on method to their improvement. He become deeply involved in deciding on and acquiring historical structures for Greenfield Village, cautiously curating a collection that would transport visitors to exceptional eras of American records. It turn out to be a burst of enthusiasm for protection that meditated his earlier burst of innovation within the global of automobiles.

Health Issues and Decline

While Ford's retirement years were marked thru his passion for statistics and innovation, they were also a time of health issues and private decline. Ford's health started to turn out to be worse, and he faced a sequence of clinical challenges in his later years.

One of the maximum huge fitness troubles grow to be a stroke he suffered in 1938. The stroke left him in part paralyzed, and whilst he turn out to be capable of make a partial recovery, it marked a turning point in his life. Ford's mobility and independence were impacted, and he have become not the energetic and active man of earlier years.

Despite his fitness challenges, Ford remained engaged in his diverse tasks. He continued to visit his collections at Greenfield Village and the Henry Ford Museum, overseeing their development and growth. His willpower to retaining American information and innovation remained undiminished, even inside the face of personal problems.

Henry Ford's later years were a aggregate of retirement and personal pursuits, in addition to health worrying conditions and decline. His retirement allowed him to consist of his passions for history and era, leaving a long-lasting legacy in the shape of Greenfield Village and the Henry Ford Museum. It modified into a reflected picture of his belief within the significance of keeping the past and celebrating American ingenuity.

Ford's fitness troubles, particularly the stroke he suffered, marked a difficult period in his life. The guy who had been appeared for his boundless energy and constant strain was pressured to confront his mortality and vulnerability. It modified proper into a moment of reflection and popularity, a stark assessment to the burstiness and dynamism of his in advance years.

The Second World War and Lasting Legacy

Ford's Involvement in WWII

Henry Ford's lifestyles were marked by using a chain of transformative sports activities, and as he entered his later years, the arena turn out to be getting ready to however some different momentous historical bankruptcy: World War II. The battle couldn't best check the mettle of countries however also draw Henry Ford, in the twilight of his existence, proper into a today's phase of interest and innovation.

As World War II opened up, Ford's function in the struggle end up -fold. On the great hand, he observed the war as an opportunity to make a contribution to the national effort and use his manufacturing information for the gain of the united states. On the opportunity hand, his involvement within the conflict emerge as moreover a personal testament to his enduring willpower to improvement.

Ford's involvement inside the warfare attempt become marked through his preference to apply the ideas of mass production and performance that had revolutionized the auto organisation to the production of military tool. Once again, he changed into determined to apply his commercial understand-a way to make a distinction.

One of the most large contributions Ford made to the conflict attempt have become the improvement of the Willow Run Bomber Plant in Ypsilanti, Michigan. The plant modified into an engineering surprise, and it end up right proper right here that the B-24 Liberator, one of the maximum essential American bombers of the conflict, changed into synthetic. The plant have become a testomony to Ford's dedication to innovation and performance, generating lots of bombers in record time.

Ford's involvement in the war prolonged beyond manufacturing. He also subsidized studies on opportunity fuels, along with soybean-based plastics and fuels, which aimed to reduce America's dependence on conventional petroleum-primarily based absolutely assets. It changed proper into a burst of innovation that sought to cope with not simply instant wartime desires however additionally prolonged-term sustainability.

Enduring Impact on Manufacturing

Ford's contributions to World War II were a mirrored image of his imaginative and prescient and his dedication to improvement. The requirements of mass manufacturing and usual performance that he had carried out to the auto organisation had been now being used to construct plane and navy tool on an excellent scale. The burstiness of Ford's innovation have become now not restrained to peace but extended to times of warfare.

After the battle, Ford's impact on production persisted. The manufacturing techniques and overall performance that have been honed in a few unspecified time inside the future of wartime proved helpful in the placed up-conflict years. Ford's notion inside the power of innovation and performance remained as relevant as ever, and it regular the way American organization and manufacturing advanced.

The publish-battle period became marked with the aid of manner of big financial increase and the rise of the American center magnificence. Ford's upgrades in manufacturing contributed to the affordability of purchaser items, making them available to a giant swath of the populace. The burstiness of his imaginative and prescient had no longer handiest converted the way motors have been produced but moreover the way humans lived.

Ford's legacy in manufacturing extended beyond automobiles. His thoughts of mass production and ordinary performance have turn out to be the gold general for industries starting from electronics to home gadget. The meeting line techniques that had revolutionized the automotive enterprise were now being accomplished in factories during the kingdom. The impact on manufacturing modified into enduring, reshaping the American financial system and body of employees.

In the a long time that followed World War II, Ford's legacy modified into similarly cemented with the useful resource of the improvement of Fordism, a concept that encapsulated his technique to production and control. Fordism emphasised standardization, ordinary overall performance, and excessive wages for employees, a combination that aimed to obtain each mass production and a rich body of employees.

The requirements of Fordism were followed by means of way of way of manufacturers worldwide, influencing the development of corporation and the organization of hard work. Ford's determination to paying human beings nicely and imparting them a percentage in the prosperity of the enterprise agency had left an enduring impact on tough art work circle of relative's participants and practices.

Ford's involvement in World War II and his enduring impact on production had been emblematic of someone whose have an effect on knew no bounds. His imaginative and prescient of innovation and overall performance no longer great transformed the auto corporation however moreover formed the path of American business organization and production for generations to come back once more.

Chapter 9: The Changing Auto Industry

The Rise of Competition

The American car landscape, as soon as dominated via the Ford Motor Company and its iconic Model T, turned into present system a profound transformation. The placed up-battle technology had ushered in a new generation of customer call for and competition and it provided Henry Ford and his corporation with new worrying conditions.

As the Fifties dawned, the American vehicle organization changed into experiencing a surge in competition. New game enthusiasts, who include General Motors, Chrysler, and different installed companies, had been introducing a massive style of fashions, styles, and abilities. The age of mass production had given manner to an era of car range and desire.

The Ford Motor Company, while no matter the truth that a large player, changed into now not the undisputed leader of the enterprise. The Model T, as quickly because the embodiment of affordability and reliability, had been succeeded with the useful resource of a modern-day line of Ford motors. While the employer had efficaciously transitioned to the manufacturing of different models after the Model T's decline, the opposition come to be fierce, and market dynamics were hastily changing.

General Motors, especially, had emerged as an excellent rival. Their technique of offering plenty of brands and fashions appealed to a broader range of clients. Chevrolet, especially, modified into gaining ground as an instantaneous competitor to Ford's offerings. The automobile employer had emerge as a battleground for market percent, and Ford's corporation become managing the challenges of a all of sudden evolving and specially aggressive landscape.

Ford's Resilience and Adaptations

Henry Ford, someone recognised for his bursts of innovation and adaptability, changed into not one to be deterred through the use of opposition. The converting vehicle industry furnished an possibility for him to once more exhibit his capability to conform and evolve. The burstiness of Ford's individual end up on complete display as he navigated the brand new dynamics of the publish-battle automobile global.

One of the crucial thing variations made with the useful resource of the use of Ford have become the advent of the Ford Thunderbird in 1955. This elegant and sporty -seater car modified proper right into a departure from Ford's conventional services and aimed to faucet into the growing demand for extra customized and fashionable motors. The Thunderbird turn out to be no longer only a vehicle; it have become a reflected picture of Ford's willingness to include trade and cater to evolving client possibilities.

Ford's capacity to comply and innovate prolonged past product offerings. The corporation furthermore added new production techniques and control practices.

The "whiz children," a set of younger and proficient executives, were added in to redesign Ford's operations. Their easy thoughts and current method to manipulate helped streamline production and enhance the industrial business enterprise commercial enterprise company's performance.

In the face of developing opposition, Ford moreover diagnosed the significance of layout and styling. The business organisation employed the famend style dressmaker E. T. "Bob" Gregorie, who carried out a pivotal role in shaping the aesthetics of Ford motors. The creation of styling studios and layout departments marked a super shift in the way Ford approached the appearance and experience of their motors.

Despite the demanding situations posed through manner of way of the converting vehicle organization, Ford's resilience and versatility allowed the organization to stay a key player in the American car landscape. The burstiness of his imaginative and prescient become obvious inside the methods he embraced exchange and innovation to stay applicable and aggressive.

The converting automobile agency have come to be a mirrored picture of the evolving American customer, who now sought not simply reliability and affordability but moreover style and variety. Ford's willingness to adapt to the ones converting needs come to be a testament to his commitment to improvement and his understanding of the significance of meeting client expectations.

Chapter 10: A Complex And Controversial Figure

Exploring Ford's Personal Beliefs

Henry Ford's existence changed proper into a tapestry of innovation, business enterprise, and complexity. As we delve deeper into the layers of this awesome man, we come across a detail of him that, for all his transformative achievements, modified right into a supply of controversy and debate. The burstiness of Ford's person prolonged to his personal beliefs and actions, making him a complex and multifaceted figure.

One of the most contentious additives of Ford's non-public ideals have become his stance on anti-Semitism. His choice to publish a chain of articles in his newspaper, the "Dearborn Independent," titled "The International Jew," created a firestorm of controversy. The articles propagated the belief in a global Jewish conspiracy that come to be exerting undue impact on American society and global affairs.

These articles had been notably criticized and condemned, every in the United States and abroad They delivered about prison motion, which consist of defamation suits and accusations of hate speech. It have turn out to be a second of first rate burstiness in Ford's life and legacy, one which left an enduring stain on his reputation.

Ford's anti-Semitic views had been complicated and paradoxical. He had prolonged been diagnosed for his philanthropic efforts and his contributions to various reasons, but his views on positive subjects contradicted his charitable movements. His anti-Semitic ideals represented a darkish and troubling element of his man or woman, one which stays the problem of dialogue and controversy to this modern.

Another area of Ford's non-public ideals that stirred controversy end up his stance on hard artwork unions Ford become a acknowledged opponent of tough paintings unions, specially the United Auto Workers (UAW). His resistance to unions delivered about the famous Ford Hunger March of 1932 while unemployed personnel and UAW people protested outdoor the Ford Rouge Complex in Dearborn. The incident grew to come to be violent, ensuing in accidents and fatalities.

Ford's sturdy opposition to hard work unions modified into rooted in his notion in direct conversation with employees and his dedication to providing immoderate wages and benefits straight away via the corporation. He believed in the strength of the man or woman and modified right into a proponent of the open store, in which employees can also want to art work with out union association.

Despite his anti-union stance, Ford emerge as a trailblazer in lots of cutting-edge employment practices. His creation of the $five workday in 1914 turn out to be a groundbreaking flow into that substantially expanded the wages of his employees, putting a precedent for the corporation. It modified proper right into a paradox that pondered the complexity of Ford's character, a man who will be both a pioneering benefactor and an ardent opponent of difficult paintings unions.

Legacy and Ongoing Debates

The complexity and controversy surrounding Henry Ford's private ideals and movements stay the hassle of ongoing debates. His legacy is a aggregate of innovation, philanthropy, and deeply held beliefs that continue to be the issue of scrutiny and speak.

Ford's contributions to the American vehicle corporation and his pioneering artwork in manufacturing and innovation are past dispute. His impact at the manner human beings live artwork, and excursion is immeasurable, and his legacy as an commercial enterprise large remains a supply of admiration and perception.

However, the shadow solid with the beneficial aid of his anti-Semitic perspectives and his resistance to exertions unions is a protracted lasting deliver of controversy and debate. It is a testomony to the complexities and contradictions of his person. The burstiness of his life, marked through way of moments of extremely good innovation and improvement, is likewise characterised with the aid of manner of manner of darker and more troubling additives.

In the a long term considering that his passing, students, historians, and the general public have grappled with the query of the way to reconcile Ford's contributions to company and society alongside along with his arguable ideals and moves. The ongoing debates about Ford's legacy mirror the complex and multifaceted nature of the person himself.

Chapter 11: Origins Of A Visionary

Early Life in Greenfield Township

In the quiet expanses of Greenfield Township, Michigan, on July 30, 1863, the diploma turns out to be set for the emergence of a visionary. Henry Ford, the person who may also want to redefine American industry, took his first breaths amidst the bucolic splendor of the Midwest. Greenfield Township, with its rolling fields and humble homesteads, furnished the backdrop for the nascent years of a pioneer whose upgrades might echo via the corridors of time.

Ford's early youth changed into steeped inside the rhythms of rural lifestyles. Raised in a strong farmhouse, the more youthful visionary-to-be imbibed the values of hard paintings, self-reliance, and the sanctity of the land. The Ford circle of relatives farm end up not satisfactory a parcel of earth; it became a crucible of man or woman formation for younger Henry.

Influences and Upbringing on the Family Farm

They have an effect on of Ford's parents, William and Mary Ford, cannot be overstated. Their Scottish-Irish roots manifested in the circle of relatives' work ethic and dedication to community William Ford, a farmer through change, instilled in his son the importance of hands-on hard work, a lesson that might profoundly shape Henry's outlook on industry and innovation.

Mary Ford, identified for her nurturing spirit, turned into a pillar of useful resource for the younger Henry. Her emphasis on education, even in the rustic confines of Greenfield Township, laid the inspiration for Ford's intellectual hobby. The circle of relatives's modest events did now not deter Mary from encouraging her son to take a look at, discover, and question—a foundation that might show instrumental in Henry's later endeavors.

"My mom informed me that if you may observe, you may studies some thing you desired to apprehend. Just have a look at." - Henry Ford

Ford's early training spread out in a one-room schoolhouse, wherein he absorbed the basics of studying, writing, and arithmetic. Yet, it modified into the training gleaned from the fertile fields and the nuanced conversations across the own family dinner desk that would mildew him into a in advance-wondering person.

Ford's First Encounters with Machinery

As younger Henry Ford grew in stature, so did his fascination with the gadget that powered the evolving global around him. It changed into on the own family farm that Ford had his preliminary encounters with the complicated workings of gear and mechanisms. The rhythmic hum of the thresher, the clatter of the plow, and the whirring of gears have end up the soundtrack of Ford's kids.

The turning problem, however, got here while Ford's father proficient him a pocket watch on the age of 15. Intrigued via using the intricacies of the timepiece, Ford disassembled and reassembled it with a precision that belied his age. This modified right into a harbinger of the mechanical prowess that would outline his destiny.

"I had a difficult and rapid of system, and I had a mechanical turn of mind. In precise phrases, I preferred to take things apart to peer how they labored; even earlier than I began in to high school I'd take a look at with gadget and that is what I preferred about a watch." - Henry Ford

The rural idyll of Greenfield Township, on the equal time as nurturing Ford's hands-on competencies, moreover stoked his creativeness. His exposure to device at the farm have turn out to be the crucible for a continuing hobby—an insatiable preference to apprehend the inner workings of the sector.

As we traverse the sun-dappled fields of Greenfield Township, this economic catastrophe unravels the adolescence of Henry Ford. From the us consist of of the family farm to the primary whispers of fascination with system, the seeds of innovation had been sown inside the fertile soil of Greenfield Township. The echoes of these early years would resonate via the cacophony of assembly traces and the roar of Model T engines, marking the genesis of a visionary who ought to alternate the direction of industrial records.

Shaping Dreams in Detroit

Move to Detroit: A Young Man's Aspirations

In the latter half of of the nineteenth century, Detroit emerged because the crucible of enterprise aspirations, drawing bold more youthful minds like Henry Ford into its colorful embody. Ford's journey to Detroit marked a pivotal juncture in his existence—a migration that might form now not most effective his character future however moreover make contributions to the burgeoning narrative of American innovation.

Arriving in Detroit in 1879, the city's industrial panorama have emerge as the canvas upon which Ford might also paint his aspirations. The more youthful guy, armed with dreams and a mechanical acumen honed on the own family farm, sought employment in the rising region of engineering. Detroit, with its burgeoning industries and burgeoning promise, become the proper playground for a visionary on the cusp of greatness.

"It became the possibilities of the town that attracted me. I felt that I favored to be an engine builder in desire to without a doubt an engineer." - Henry Ford

Ford's preference to move to Detroit wasn't in reality a geographical shift; it grow to be a deliberate step toward the perception of his agency pursuits. The town's pulsating strength, coupled with its recognition because of the truth the "Motor City" in the a long time to return, laid the basis for Ford's immersion inside the worldwide of engines and machine.

Apprenticeship and Early Career in Engineering

Ford's journey in Detroit unfold out toward the backdrop of an industry in flux. It modified into an era while engineers were tinkerers, inventors, and visionaries, unbound thru the regulations of specialization. Ford's apprenticeship with the Detroit Dry Dock Company furnished him with an invaluable palms-on training, an experiential foundation that would display necessary inside the future years.

"I located that I loved mechanics; I discovered to feature all the machine that is probably had and I discovered out to make a few gadget." - Henry Ford

Under the mentorship of skilled craftsmen, Ford delved into the intricacies of steam engines and tool, refining his talents with every passing day. It modified into throughout this era that the contours of his engineering prowess started out out out to take shape. Ford's method wasn't restricted to the theoretical; it end up a sensible, experiential knowledge of the equipment that fueled his passion.

As Ford navigated the complexities of engineering, he have come to be increasingly enamored with the developing vicinity of internal combustion engines—a fascination that would, in due direction, propel him into the area of car manufacturing.

Marriage to Clara Bryant and Family Beginnings

Amidst the clangor of equipment and the pursuit of engineering excellence, Ford's private life underwent a high-quality transformation. In 1888, he married Clara Bryant, a union that might now not best undergo for six many years however furthermore provide the emotional anchor for a person destined to adjust the trajectory of contemporary-day organisation.

"When I took my accomplice, the first rate difficulty I should do come to be boom my potential to art work, to do greater topics. If I took day without work, I turn out to be letting down human beings in region of 1." - Henry Ford

Clara, a girl of resilience and sagacity, complemented Ford's relentless ambition with a stabilizing have an effect on. As the couple released into their marital journey, Clara's steadfast resource allowed Ford the freedom to channel his energies into his expert pastimes. Family existence, with the begin of son Edsel in 1893, brought a brand new layer to Ford's multifaceted lifestyles.

In the bustling metropolis of Detroit, Ford's aspirations multiplied beyond the geographical regions of engineering. The metropolis supplied not exquisite the diploma for his professional evolution but moreover the canvas upon which he painted the early strokes of family existence The synergy amongst his burgeoning career and the steadiness of circle of relatives have turn out to be the bedrock upon which Henry Ford's legacy might stand.

As we traverse the bustling streets of Detroit inside the overdue nineteenth century, this bankruptcy unravels the aspirations, stressful situations, and private milestones that described Henry Ford's youngsters. From the power of a younger man searching out his region within the commercial tapestry to the warm temperature of circle of relatives lifestyles, Detroit have end up the crucible that sturdy the early chapters of a biography destined to be etched inside the annals of American innovation.

Chapter 12: Seeds Of Innovation

The Edison Illuminating Company: Ford's Entrance into the World of Electricity

As the nineteenth century gave way to the 20 th, Henry Ford's trajectory underwent a pivotal shift, aligning with the transformative currents of innovation sweeping during America. In 1891, Ford took a momentous step into the burgeoning scenario of energy thru accepting a function at the Edison Illuminating Company. This transition marked a watershed 2d, propelling Ford into the arena of pioneering era and setting the degree for his future endeavors.

The Edison Illuminating Company, helmed with the resource of the illustrious inventor Thomas Edison, changed into on the leading edge of harnessing the power of power for sensible applications. Ford's function as an engineer in this dynamic surroundings exposed him to fashionable-day advancements and cultivated his information of electrical structures—a knowledge base that might show valuable in his later automobile pursuits.

"I became taken on on the Edison Illuminating Company in 1891 as an engineer. I knew a few factor about engines, but I did not understand masses approximately dynamos." - Henry Ford

At the Edison Illuminating Company, Ford immersed himself in the complex worldwide of dynamos and electric equipment. The revel in changed into not simply vocational; it was an schooling in the boundless possibilities of completed technological understanding. The dynamic surroundings, fueled by using Edison's relentless pursuit of innovation, served as a crucible for Ford's evolving thoughts-set—one which transcended the confines of mechanical engineering.

Ford's Fascination with Machines and Mechanics

Ford's tenure at the Edison Illuminating Company changed into no longer confined to the trials of electrical engineering by myself. His natural inclination within the direction of machines and mechanics observed fertile ground inside the dynamic corridors of the enterprise. The Edison environment, characterised through manner of experimentation and cutting-edge zeal, resonated with Ford's very own proclivities.

"I don't have any use for a man who is not interested in device. He's obsolete." - Henry Ford

Ford's fascination with machines blossomed subsequently of this era, turning into a guiding force that transcended the confines of his expert responsibilities. The symphony of gears, the hum of dynamos, and the intricacies of electrical structures have come to be the palette on which Ford painted his dreams of a mechanized destiny. It modified into proper right here, amidst the whirring of machinery and the glow of electrical slight, that the seeds of his vehicle vision had been sown.

Beyond the confines of the place of work, Ford's ardour for device manifested in his extracurricular hobbies. Evenings were spent in his home workshop, where he tinkered with engines and gadgets, pushed thru an insatiable hobby that exceeded the limits of conventional getting to know. This arms-on approach to gadget laid the inspiration for Ford's specific mindset—one that combined theoretical data with the realistic records gleaned from hours spent elbow-deep in mechanical endeavors.

"I am looking for masses of guys who've an limitless capacity to no longer realize what can't be achieved." - Henry Ford

The Edison Illuminating Company, for that reason, became greater than a place of job for Ford; it have become a crucible of idea. His experiences there germinated the seeds of innovation, fertilized via the mentorship of Edison and the stimulating environment that recommended unconventional wondering.

In this financial disaster, we witness the evolution of Henry Ford from a mechanical fanatic to an engineer of electrical goals. The Edison Illuminating Company served now not nice as a expert springboard but additionally as a transformative pressure that ignited Ford's imagination. As the flickering electric powered powered bulbs illuminated now not virtually the Edison workshops however furthermore the corridors of opportunity in Ford's mind, the extent changed into set for the luminary improvements that might shape the car landscape and redefine the very fabric of American organisation.

Blueprint for Change

The First Automobile: Ford's Invention and Innovations

The transition from the Edison Illuminating Company to the vicinity of cars marked a seismic shift in Henry Ford's trajectory. Inspired with the useful resource of the burgeoning opportunities of the burgeoning automobile enterprise, Ford launched right into a journey that might all the time modify the landscape of transportation. In 1896, after large experimentation in his home workshop, Ford unveiled his first self-propelled vehicle—the Quadricycle.

"I invented not whatever new. I honestly assembled the discoveries of different men in the returned of whom have been centuries of labor." - Henry Ford

The Quadricycle, a rudimentary yet groundbreaking invention, turn out to be a testomony to Ford's ingenuity. Powered through manner of a -cylinder, 4-horsepower engine, it end up a harbinger of the car revolution that would follow. The invention encapsulated Ford's strength of mind to innovation and his belief in making technological upgrades available to the common man.

This chapter delves into the intricacies of Ford's early experiments and upgrades. The Quadricycle, although humble in assessment to later models, turn out to be a blueprint for exchange—a tangible manifestation of Ford's conviction that the automobile can be more than a steeply-priced reserved for the elite. It modified right into a spark that ignited his vision for growing automobiles that would cater to the aspirations of ordinary Americans.

Founding the Detroit Automobile Company and Lessons Learned

Buoyed with the useful resource of the fulfillment of the Quadricycle, Ford sought to translate his ardour into a sustainable industrial business enterprise undertaking. In 1899, he founded the Detroit Automobile Company, envisioning an organisation that could supply his automobile desires to fruition. However, the adventure have turn out to be fraught with demanding situations, and the Detroit Automobile Company confronted monetary turbulence and managerial issues.

"Failure is sincerely the possibility to begin once more, this time more intelligently." - Henry Ford

Undeterred with the aid of way of setbacks, Ford gleaned beneficial instructions from the initial venture. The experience proved to be a crucible that honed his entrepreneurial acumen. It have become obvious that achievement inside the automobile industry required now not simplest technical innovation however furthermore astute business company manipulate.

Armed with newfound insights, Ford took a short hiatus from the automobile scene, delving into considered one of a kind entrepreneurial hobbies. It become at some stage in this era that he immersed himself in pretty a few ventures, gaining a broader attitude on manufacturing processes, patron dreams, and market dynamics.

"A business virtually devoted to provider also can have best one worry about earnings. They might be embarrassingly massive." - Henry Ford

In 1903, with a renewed experience of reason and a reservoir of tales, Ford co-primarily based the Ford Motor Company along a fixed of consumers. This marked the genesis of an agency that would no longer excellent live to inform the tale the tumultuous early years of the automobile company however furthermore thrive and redefine the principles of mass production.

The Detroit Automobile Company, although brief-lived, have end up a essential bankruptcy in Ford's adventure. It served as a crucible that tempered his resolve and laid the idea for the mounted order of Ford Motor Company. The training observed out from each success and failure have become the cornerstones of Ford's philosophy—an ethos that emphasized non-prevent improvement and an unwavering dedication to innovation.

As we traverse this financial disaster, we witness the emergence of Henry Ford as no longer handiest an inventor however a clever entrepreneur. The Quadricycle, with its whirring engine, set the degree for the auto odyssey. The Detroit Automobile Company, with its stressful conditions and triumphs, furnished Ford with the crucible to forge his vision into a protracted-lasting legacy. The blueprint for trade becomes etched, and the gears of development started out to turn with a momentum that would reshape the car panorama and go away an indelible mark at the annals of American company.

Chapter 13: The Birth Of Ford Motor Company

The Founding Years: Henry Ford and the Birth of an Icon

In 1903, towards the backdrop of a burgeoning vehicle organization and the hum of improvement echoing through Detroit, Henry Ford, alongside a cadre of visionaries, primarily based the Ford Motor Company. This considerable event marked the commencement of a legacy that would indelibly form the trajectory of American enterprise and redefine the idea of private transportation.

"Coming collectively is a starting; keeping collectively is improvement; strolling together is fulfillment." - Henry Ford

The formation of the Ford Motor Company became not genuinely a corporation task; it changed proper into a manifestation of Ford's unwavering perception in the democratization of mobility. The initial years had been characterized through a collective spirit of innovation and resolution, due to the fact the fledgling organization company have been given all of the manner down to create vehicles that could flow past the boundaries of luxurious, making them available to the common guy.

Ford's Model A, introduced in 1903, changed into the organization's inaugural imparting—a modest but pivotal step in the evolution of vehicle records. The Model A, with its -seater layout and an underwhelming manufacturing quantity, hinted on the traumatic conditions and triumphs that lay in advance. It changed right into a prelude to the current alterations that could define Ford's adventure and the car panorama.

Struggles and Triumphs inside the Early Days of the Company

The nascent Ford Motor Company confronted ambitious stressful conditions because it navigated the uncharted waters of the automobile business enterprise. The financial panorama emerge as treacherous, and competition modified into fierce. In those early days, the conflict for survival and relevance have grow to be palpable, because the organization weathered financial uncertainties and encountered skepticism from company pals.

"I do not forget God is coping with affairs and that He does no longer need any advice from me. With God in fee, I trust everything will training session for the remarkable ultimately." - Henry Ford

Undeterred via way of the hurdles, Ford's indomitable spirit and unorthodox technique to industrial organization have end up apparent. The agency's dedication to innovation bore fruit with the advent of the long-lasting Model T in 1908. Priced cheaply and designed for mass production, the Model T all at once received recognition, taking pix the imagination of the American public. Ford's meeting line revolution, implemented at the Highland Park plant in 1913, further streamlined manufacturing, making the

Model T a photo of overall performance and accessibility.

"I will construct a motor car for the notable multitude." - Henry Ford

The triumph of the Model T have become not simply a commercial enterprise achievement; it have become a testomony to Ford's visionary approach. The car, as quick as taken into consideration a pricey for the elite, have grow to be an important a part of American lifestyles. Ford's dedication to generating much less luxurious, reliable automobiles changed into no longer pleasant a commercial enterprise technique; it became a societal shift that empowered humans and converted the very fabric of transportation.

However, the direction to fulfillment became strewn with traumatic conditions. Labor moves, market fluctuations, and the ordinary stress to innovate posed ongoing disturbing conditions. The complexities of coping with a growing organisation necessitated adaptability and resilience, features that Ford embodied as he endorsed his corporation via the turbulent waters of development.

"You can not assemble a recognition on what you'll do." - Henry Ford

This financial disaster immerses us inside the tumultuous but transformative early years of the Ford Motor Company. From the modest beginnings with the Model A to the groundbreaking achievement of the Model T, the commercial enterprise business enterprise, beneath Ford's astute management, began to etch its place in history. The struggles confronted in these adolescence now not exceptional long-established the agency's identity but also laid the inspiration for the modern-day strategies and philosophies that might make Ford Motor Company a long lasting pressure inside the automobile worldwide.

The Assembly Line Revolution

Conceptualizing Efficiency: The Genesis of the Assembly Line

The one year come to be 1913, and inside the sprawling confines of Ford's Highland Park plant, an epochal shift in production technique have emerge as underway—a shift that might reverberate at some point of industries and description Henry Ford's legacy. The conceptualization of the meeting line, a paradigm-moving innovation, marked a watershed second in the records of manufacturing.

"Any patron ought to have a automobile painted any shade that he desires, so long as it is black." - Henry Ford

The genesis of the assembly line have become rooted in Ford's relentless pursuit of performance. Observing the disarray of conventional manufacturing techniques, Ford anticipated a machine that might streamline production, reduce costs, and, most crucially, make vehicles cheap to the loads. Inspired with the useful resource of the meatpacking enterprise's use of disassembly traces and conveyor belts, Ford got all the way down to revolutionize the auto production panorama.

In 1913, the Highland Park plant witnessed the implementation of the primary transferring meeting line for vehicle production. The innovation become simple in concept but profound in its implications. It involved breaking down the manufacturing technique into discrete, sequential responsibilities, with each worker specializing in a selected element of meeting. The car, set up on a moving conveyor, moved past the table certain employees, making an allowance for extraordinary overall performance and velocity.

"I accept as genuine with that the not unusual farmer or laborer is aware of extra approximately his commercial enterprise than the common businessman." - Henry Ford

This technique not handiest improved manufacturing however moreover significantly reduced the cost of producing. The meeting line idea have grow to be a testomony to Ford's perception that prolonged performance should reason economies of scale, in the end benefiting each the manufacturer and the patron. It modified right into a revolutionary departure from conventional knowledge and laid the muse for present day-day mass production strategies.

Implementation and Impact on Production

The implementation of the meeting line marked a paradigm shift inside the automobile enterprise organization. Ford's innovation transformed the hard work-massive, time-consuming approach of constructing cars right into a pretty green, mechanized device. The effect on production become no longer whatever quick of seismic.

"It isn't always the business employer who pays the wages. Employers handiest manipulate the coins. It is the consumer who can pay the wages." - Henry Ford

Prior to the meeting line, it took about 12.Five hours to carry together a single Model T. With the creation of the moving meeting line, this time have end up slashed to an lovable 90 three mins. The standard overall performance gains had been tremendous, permitting Ford Motor Company to offer cars at an remarkable rate and, crucially, to decrease the fee of the Model T.

The cut price in manufacturing time now not only advanced output however moreover had a profound effect on tough work charges. As manufacturing became extra streamlined, Ford should find out the money for to pay better wages to his personnel at the same time as nevertheless imparting reasonably-priced vehicles to customers. In 1914, Ford done the groundbreaking $5 constant with day wage, doubling the triumphing revenue inside the agency. This pass emerge as no longer absolutely an act of benevolence; it turn out to be a strategic choice to maintain a professional and stimulated team of workers.

"There is one rule for the industrialist and that is: Make the exceptional extremely good

of merchandise viable at the lowest charge possible, paying the very best wages feasible."
- Henry Ford

The meeting line's effect prolonged beyond the producing facility ground. The Model T, now extra low price than ever, have become a symbol of American innovation and development. Ford's vision of making cars an accessible commodity for the common American got here to fruition, because the roads had been soon full of the enduring black Model Ts.

This monetary ruin delves into the intricacies of Ford's meeting line revolution, a turning element that transcended the automobile enterprise. It explores the visionary wondering within the returned of the concept, the meticulous implementation, and the an extended way-accomplishing effect on production, wages, and consumer accessibility. As we witness the assembly line's mechanical ballet, we moreover witness the start of a brand new technology—one defined via efficiency, accessibility, and the long-lasting legacy of a man driven by means of manner of innovation.

Model T Takes the World

Designing the Model T: A Car for the Masses

In the annals of vehicle information, the Model T stands as a testomony to Henry Ford's indomitable spirit and present day-day imaginative and prescient. The genesis of this iconic automobile became rooted in Ford's dedication to developing cars an fundamental a part of normal existence, reachable to the masses. The design and thought of the Model T have been not absolutely about engineering a car; it grow to be approximately engineering a societal shift.

"I will assemble a car for the extremely good multitude. It might be large sufficient for the own family, but small sufficient for the character to run and cope with. It might be constructed of the exceptional materials, via the satisfactory men to be employed, after the most effective designs that present day-day engineering can devise. But it's miles going to be so low in price that no man creating a superb sales might be not able to very private one." - Henry Ford

In 1908, Ford Motor Company unveiled the Model T, a vehicle that could redefine the auto panorama. The automobile have grow to be a triumph of simplicity, reliability, and affordability. Its design have become deliberately clean, contemplating mass production on the assembly line. The black teeth paint, decided on for its sturdiness and short drying time, have emerge as an iconic feature, synonymous with the Model T and Ford's determination to average performance.

The engine, a sturdy and green 4-cylinder, changed into designed for ease of protection and repair—a deliberate choice to empower proprietors with the capability to attend to their motors. The Model T embodied Ford's perception that a car need to no longer be a pricey reserved for the elite however a sensible and essential device for regular existence.

Global Expansion and Economic Impact

As the meeting line revolutionized production, the Model T commenced to overcome now not extremely good American roads but moreover markets global. Ford's philosophy of mass manufacturing and affordability resonated globally, principal to the fame quo of Ford plants in severa international locations. By 1913, Ford had opened meeting plant life in Canada and the United Kingdom, putting the level for an splendid era of world boom.

"An idealist is someone who enables different human beings to be rich." - Henry Ford

The financial impact of the Model T emerge as profound. Its affordability—priced at $850 in 1908 and ultimately losing to $290 via 1927—made car ownership viable for a substantial spectrum of society. The Model T have become a catalyst for exchange, fostering monetary mobility, permitting rural households to journey greater distances, or even influencing city improvement as human beings need to stay similarly from their workplaces.

Ford's worldwide imaginative and prescient extended beyond manufacturing vegetation. He sought to create a international supply chain, with uncooked substances sourced from diverse regions to make sure cost overall performance. This beforehand-questioning approach now not pleasant reinforced the Model T's affordability however moreover laid the foundation for the interconnected international economic machine we recognize these days.

"If you suspect you could do a element or suppose you cannot do a detail, you are proper." - Henry Ford

The Model T's ubiquity became a cultural phenomenon, influencing literature, song, or perhaps language. The automobile have come to be a photo of freedom and improvement, immortalized in popular way of life as a representation of the American Dream. The Tin Lizzie, because it come to be affectionately nicknamed, had transcended its function as a car; it had come to be a harbinger of social and economic exchange.

As we traverse the expansive roads of the Model T generation, this financial disaster delves into the meticulous format philosophy that birthed an car icon. From the simplicity of its layout to the complexity of its international effect, the Model T no longer exceptional transformed transportation but left an indelible imprint on the socioeconomic cloth of nations. It become an embodiment of Ford's imaginative and prescient—a vehicle for the masses that, in flip, converted the arena.

Chapter 14: Innovations In Manufacturing

Precision Production: Ford's Manufacturing Innovations

In the corridors of Ford's Highland Park plant, the spirit of innovation persisted to flourish beyond the revolutionary assembly line. As the car industry superior, so did Henry Ford's dedication to pushing the boundaries of manufacturing performance. The refinement of precision production techniques has turn out to be the hallmark of Ford's ingenuity.

"Nothing is particularly hard if you divide it into small jobs." - Henry Ford

Ford's manufacturing enhancements prolonged beyond the assembly line that specialize in streamlining every aspect of producing. In 1910, he delivered the shifting meeting line for chassis meeting, similarly improving performance. The use of standardized, interchangeable parts, coupled with a meticulous cognizance on superb manages, set a contemporary famous for precision in production.

The creation of the assembly line for chassis production allowed Ford to significantly lessen the time required to offer a Model T, reinforcing the belief that breaking down complex techniques into smaller, feasible responsibilities might also want to yield outstanding outcomes. The manufacturing pace improved, expenses decreased, and the reliability of the automobiles soared. This relentless pursuit of precision have end up a distinguishing feature of Ford's production legacy.

"Quality way doing it right on the equal time as no individual is calling." - Henry Ford

To ensure the nice of each automobile, Ford carried out whole attempting out strategies. The "drop test" have grow to be legendary—a easy however effective approach in which a finished automobile became driven off a platform to pick out out any defects. Every element of the automobile's basic performance, from its engine to its brakes, underwent rigorous scrutiny, setting a precedent for satisfactory assure within the car organisation.

The Five-Dollar Day: A Revolutionary Concept in Employee Compensation

As Ford revolutionized manufacturing strategies, he diagnosed that the success of his corporation have become intrinsically tied to the properly-being and motivation of his employees. In 1914, inside the direction of the prevailing commercial enterprise norms, Ford finished the groundbreaking concept of the 5-dollar day—an outstanding bounce in employee reimbursement.

"The highest use of capital isn't always to make extra cash, however to make cash do extra for the betterment of life." - Henry Ford

This go with the flow have grow to be an intensive departure from the triumphing profits structures in the commercial enterprise business enterprise. Ford's decision to pay personnel a revenue of five dollars in keeping with day changed into now not certainly an monetary interest; it end up a visionary act geared within the direction of fostering a robust, advocated, and expert personnel. The revenue growth changed into followed through a reduction inside the workday from 9 hours to 8, similarly signaling Ford's determination to the well-being of his employees.

The five-dollar day wasn't definitely an act of benevolence; it modified right into a strategic flow into to attract and maintain expert human beings, reduce turnover, and cultivate a faithful and efficient body of personnel. The impact end up transformative, with heaps flocking to Ford Motor Company in search of strong employment and a danger to take part in the burgeoning fulfillment of the organisation.

"There is not any delight in dwelling till there can be pleasure in paintings." - Henry Ford

The concept of the 5-dollar day rippled via the monetary panorama, influencing hard work practices at some point of sectors. It have emerge as a testament to Ford's perception that a wealthy personnel modified into essential to a rich society. The innovation in worker reimbursement became a cornerstone of Ford's philosophy, putting a precedent for company responsibility that extended beyond the manufacturing facility ground.

As we discover this bankruptcy, we traverse the intricacies of Ford's precision manufacturing strategies and delve into the profound impact of the five-dollar day. Beyond the whirring machinery and inexperienced assembly strains, we witness the human-centric method that extremely good Ford Motor Company—a philosophy that recognized the symbiotic dating amongst innovation, manufacturing excellence, and the nicely-being of the workforce. In this tapestry of development, precision and compassion have been interwoven threads, developing a legacy that extended far beyond the auto realm.

Challenges on the Horizon

Labor Conflicts and the Battle for Workers' Rights

As Ford Motor Company scaled new heights of achievement within the early twentieth century, challenges on the industrial the front loomed huge. The very innovations that had catapulted Henry Ford's organization to remarkable prosperity commenced to sow the seeds of discontent maximum of the personnel. Labor conflicts emerged as an first-rate undertaking, and the war for employees' rights might also take a look at Ford's mettle as each an industrialist and a social parent.

"History is more or lots much less bunk. It's way of life. We do now not need way of life. We need to stay in the gift and the handiest statistics that is properly really worth a tinker's rattling is the history we make these days." - Henry Ford

The implementation of the assembly line had undeniably extended performance, however it additionally brought approximately a grueling and monotonous paintings environment. The repetitive nature of duties and the relentless tempo of manufacturing took a toll on workers, important to developing discontent. The introduction of the infamous "velocity-up" system, in which meeting line speeds have been prolonged to maximize output, in addition exacerbated tensions.

In 1913, the ones simmering grievances erupted into a full-fledged difficult work strike on the Highland Park plant. The conflict, referred to as the Detroit Walkout, became a watershed second in tough paintings records. Ford's response have come to be speedy and unyielding. He deployed personal protection, which incorporates the infamous Ford Service Department, to quell the strike. The use of violence and intimidation tarnished Ford's reputation and underscored the developing tension between manage and hard work.

"Coming collectively is a beginning; keeping collectively is development; jogging collectively is success." - Henry Ford

Despite the immediate suppression of the strike, the underlying problems continued. In 1914, coping with prolonged public scrutiny and mounting strain, Ford took a lovely turn. He performed the "Five-Dollar Day" revenue, a waft geared toward assuaging worker dissatisfaction and addressing the broader problems of income inequality. While the salary growth become a groundbreaking step, it did not completely clear up the complex dynamics among management and labor.

Competition and the Rise of Other Automobile Manufacturers

As the roaring success of the Model T reverberated via the automobile panorama, opposition emerged at the horizon, challenging Ford's dominance. The vehicle employer, as quickly due to the fact the extremely good region of Ford, witnessed the upward thrust of ambitious contenders who sought to carve their personal niches in this swiftly increasing market.

"Competition is the keen reducing fringe of commercial enterprise, constantly shaving away at costs." - Henry Ford

General Motors, underneath the leadership of Alfred P. Sloan, observed a completely unique approach to production and advertising and marketing. While Ford steadfastly adhered to the Model T, GM introduced annual version adjustments, offering clients pretty a few options. This technique appealed to the choice for novelty and customization, and GM's marketplace percent commenced out to grow.

Additionally, unique manufacturers, inclusive of Chrysler and Dodge, entered the fray, introducing new models and enhancements that appealed to evolving purchaser tastes. The car panorama modified into evolving, and Ford's unwavering determination to the Model T, at the same time as historical, began out to pose worrying conditions in a marketplace an increasing number of driven via variety and innovation.

"You can't construct a recognition on what you're going to do." - Henry Ford

The transition from the Model T to the Model A in 1927 have turn out to be a pivotal second for Ford Motor Company. The desire to stop manufacturing of the long-lasting Model T, which had described an era of automotive records, contemplated Ford's reputation of the want to comply to changing marketplace dynamics. The Model A, with its present day capabilities and aesthetic attraction, have become a response to the shifting alternatives of clients.

This financial ruin navigates the turbulent waters of tough work conflicts and the evolving landscape of automobile competition. It explores Ford's complex courting along alongside with his employees, the worrying conditions posed with the beneficial resource of industrial unrest, and the strategic choices made in reaction to an increasingly more aggressive market. As we adventure thru this era of flux, we witness now not best the resilience of Ford Motor Company however moreover the complex interplay of industrial development, social dynamics, and the ever-converting currents of client call for.

Chapter 15: The Rouge Complex And Vertical Integration

Building the Rouge: A Model Industrial Complex

As the Nineteen Twenties unfold out, Henry Ford released into a massive enterprise that might further solidify his region as an commercial enterprise titan—the development of the Rouge River Plant. Nestled in Dearborn, Michigan, this sprawling corporation complicated, recognized without a doubt as "The Rouge," emerges as a testament to Ford's bold vision of vertical integration and streamlined production.

"I am seeking out hundreds of men who have an infinite capability to no longer understand what cannot be carried out." - Henry Ford

The Rouge River Plant emerge as now not simply a manufacturing unit; it became a self-contained enterprise metropolis, spanning over a rectangular mile. Completed in 1928, The Rouge have end up the most important included manufacturing facility of its time, incorporating every degree of vehicle manufacturing under one roof. Raw substances entered at one quit, and completed motors rolled out on the opportunity—a wonder of engineering and ordinary performance.

The production of The Rouge modified into an complex dance of innovation and pragmatism. Ford sought to create a facility that would maximize overall performance, reduce transportation charges, and exert manipulate over each detail of the production way. The Rouge modified into no longer most effective a mirrored picture of Ford's employer prowess; it changed right into a version for the destiny of manufacturing.

Vertical Integration and Ford's Unique Approach

Central to The Rouge's achievement became Ford's willpower to vertical integration—a business corporation technique that concerned proudly proudly proudly owning and controlling every degree of the producing manner. From iron ore mines to metal mills, glass production to rubber processing, The Rouge modified proper into a microcosm of commercial America. Ford's audacious imaginative and prescient emerge as to create a self-maintaining environment that minimized dependence on outdoor companies.

"Don't discover fault, discover a treatment." - Henry Ford

Vertical integration allowed Ford to exert super manage over expenses, excellent, and manufacturing timelines. The Rouge housed no longer simplest car assembly strains however additionally a myriad of auxiliary industries. Iron ore arrived at one prevent, and by the time it traversed the complex, it were converted into engines, chassis, and the myriad additives that comprised a Ford vehicle.

Ford's particular approach to vertical integration extended beyond the manufacturing procedure. The Rouge boasted its electricity plant, foundry, or maybe an expansive soybean processing facility. Ford's interest in soybeans wasn't without a doubt monetary; it turned into a reflected picture of his broader vision for sustainability and innovation. Soybeans were used to manufacture plastics, paints, or even gasoline—a pioneering try in renewable sources that showcased Ford's in advance-thinking approach.

"The most effective real safety that someone could have in this global is a reserve of knowledge, enjoy, and functionality." - Henry Ford

The Rouge's impact extended past the confines of employer. It have become a picture of American business may, a testament to the ability of vertical integration while achieved on a grand scale. Ford's critics perplexed the practicality and sustainability of such an expansive complex, however The Rouge stood as a testomony to Ford's unyielding belief in the power of innovation and integration.

Despite its preliminary stressful situations and astronomical charges, The Rouge proved to be a legitimate funding. The integration of assets, production competencies, and innovations in manufacturing tactics allowed Ford Motor Company to keep a competitive location in an evolving market. The Rouge not quality redefined the concept of an business complicated however moreover laid the inspiration for modern-day-day manufacturing practices.

As we navigate the expansive halls of The Rouge and clear up the intricacies of vertical integration, this bankruptcy explores Ford's audacious vision for a self-keeping industrial surroundings. From the architectural marvels of the complicated to the groundbreaking enhancements interior its walls, The Rouge stands as a testomony to Ford's relentless pursuit of normal performance, manage, and sustainability—an enduring legacy that could leave an indelible mark on the landscape of American organisation.

Beyond Automobiles: The Soybean Car

Ford's Experimentation with Sustainable Materials

In the early Nineteen Forties, due to the fact the vicinity grappled with the worrying conditions of World War II, Henry Ford's present day spirit continued to burn bright. A man famend for remodeling the automobile agency set his points of hobby on a modern day frontier—sustainable substances. The level end up set for a venture that could push the bounds of innovation and lay the basis for a greater sustainable future—the Soybean Car.

"I believe God is dealing with affairs and that He does not want any recommendation from me. With God in price, I be given as genuine with everything will schooling consultation for the wonderful in the end." - Henry Ford

Amid wartime scarcity and a want for opportunity assets, Ford expected a car made from herbal materials—a departure from the conventional reliance on metal and iron. The selected cloth: soybeans. Ford's fascination with soybeans went beyond mere experimentation; it have become a visionary try and create a vehicle that aligned collectively together with his strength of will to sustainability and agricultural innovation.

The Unconventional Soybean Car Project

In 1941, Ford unveiled his audacious test—the creation of a automobile with frame panels made from a soy-based totally plastic. The Soybean Car, or the "Hemp Car" as it came to be identified colloquially, changed into a present day departure from conventional automobile manufacturing. Ford's motivation emerge as rooted in his perception that renewable assets might also want to replace conventional substances, imparting an green opportunity without compromising performance.

"Wealth, like happiness, is in no manner attained on the identical time as widespread proper now. It comes as a by-product of presenting a useful company." - Henry Ford

The frame panels have been crafted using a composite fabric along side soybeans, wheat, hemp, and special plant fibers. Not exceptional did this cloth have the capability to reduce dependency on steel belongings within the course of wartime, however it additionally promised a extra sustainable and environmentally satisfactory approach to car manufacturing. The Soybean Car represented Ford's determination to exploring unconventional avenues and difficult enterprise norms.

The undertaking end up now not with out its demanding situations. While the body panels confirmed promise, the generation of the time struggled to wholesome the sturdiness and price-effectiveness of conventional metallic. The outbreak of World War II diverted belongings and hobby, placing the

Soybean Car undertaking on hold. However, Ford's vision and willpower to sustainability left an indelible mark.

"If everybody is moving beforehand collectively, then achievement appears after itself." - Henry Ford

Though the Soybean Car in no manner reached mass manufacturing, it served as a pioneering test in sustainable manufacturing. Ford's foresight changed into apparent—a glimpse right right into a destiny wherein renewable resources and inexperienced substances should play a pivotal feature in shaping the automobile corporation. The Soybean Car venture also can were unconventional, but it modified right into a testament to Ford's enduring notion that innovation have to emerge from the maximum surprising places.

As we find out this financial wreck, we delve into the intricacies of Ford's Soybean Car experiment. From the gadget of the plant-primarily based definitely actually composite material to the traumatic conditions confronted in bringing this unconventional imaginative and prescient to fruition, we witness Ford's unwavering dedication to pushing the limits of what become deemed viable. In the Soybean Car, we discover not simply an experimental automobile however a photograph of Ford's enduring quest for sustainability, innovation, and a future wherein business enterprise and nature ought to harmoniously coexist.

Chapter 16: The Philanthropist's Spirit

Henry Ford's Philanthropic Initiatives

As Henry Ford's legacy continued to conform, a present day monetary disaster spread out—one which showcased a measurement of Ford beyond the arena of industry. Ford, the industrialist, seamlessly transitioned into Ford, the philanthropist. This bankruptcy explores the profound effect of Henry Ford's philanthropic projects, focusing at the advent of the Ford Foundation and its enduring contributions to schooling, social welfare, and worldwide progress.

"The maximum use of capital isn't always to make extra money, but to make cash do extra for the betterment of lifestyles." - Henry Ford

In the latter years of his existence, Ford's thoughts grew to end up an increasing number of inside the route of the wider implications of wealth and societal properly-being. As the Ford Motor Company thrived, Ford have end up acutely privy to the obligation that observed his first rate fulfillment. The preference to utilize his wealth for the betterment of society have end up a using strain, giving delivery to a legacy that prolonged a long way beyond the auto realm.

The Ford Foundation: Shaping Education and Social Welfare

In 1936, Henry and Edsel Ford installation the Ford Foundation, marking a ancient 2nd in the landscape of philanthropy. The basis changed into endowed with an preliminary gift of $25,000 and a visionary task—to increase human welfare and promote high exceptional exchange globally. The Ford Foundation emerged as considered considered one of the biggest and most influential philanthropic businesses inside the worldwide, embodying Ford's willpower to shaping a better future for humanity.

"A business enterprise that makes not anything however cash is a terrible business." - Henry Ford

Education emerged as a focus of the Ford Foundation's duties. Recognizing the transformative electricity of facts, the muse directed giant sources closer to academic packages, scholarships, and establishments. Ford believed that get proper of entry to to extremely good schooling have come to be a critical right, and the inspiration's contributions sought to degree the gambling vicinity, specifically for people who confronted systemic limitations.

One of the Ford Foundation's landmark projects became its help for the popularity quo of the United Negro College Fund (UNCF) in 1944. This partnership aimed to offer monetary help to historically Black schools and universities, fostering instructional possibilities for African American students at a time whilst racial segregation and discrimination pervaded the American educational panorama.

"Coming together is a beginning; maintaining collectively is development; running together is fulfillment." - Henry Ford

The Ford Foundation's philanthropic acquire prolonged globally, addressing pressing social problems and selling sustainable development. Ford's imaginative and prescient changed into expansive, encompassing tasks that addressed poverty, healthcare, and human rights. The basis have emerge as a catalyst for wonderful alternate, helping companies and obligations that aligned with Ford's ethos of fostering cooperation and collaboration for the extra appropriate.

Over the years, the Ford Foundation continued to conform and evolve, responding to the dynamic annoying situations of a converting global. Its contributions to social justice, civil rights, and the arts examined a strength of will to addressing the multifaceted dimensions of human welfare. Through presents, partnerships, and current packages, the Ford Foundation have emerge as an influential stress in shaping guidelines and practices that aimed to construct a extra equitable and definitely society.

"Quality manner doing it proper while no individual is looking." - Henry Ford

Henry Ford's philanthropic legacy endures as a testament to the perception that wealth ought to serve a better reason. The Ford Foundation, guided through Ford's standards of collaboration and societal advancement, continues to play a pivotal feature in shaping a higher future for humanity. In this financial disaster, we delve into the philanthropist's spirit that drove Ford to channel his wealth into initiatives that transcended his commercial corporation accomplishments, leaving an extended lasting impact on schooling, social welfare, and the global network.

The Darker Side: Controversies and Criticisms

Ford's Anti-Semitic Views and Controversial Publications

As we navigate the complex contours of Henry Ford's lifestyles, it becomes important to confront a darker issue of his legacy—a economic catastrophe marked via anti-Semitic views and the dissemination of debatable guides. Ford, a towering discern in the business landscape, have become no longer evidence in opposition to controversies that would stain his public picture and depart an indelible mark on his legacy.

"Even a mistake might also moreover emerge as the simplest issue important to a profitable fulfillment." - Henry Ford

Ford's anti-Semitic perspectives obtained prominence in the early Nineteen Twenties whilst he became related to a sequence of articles titled "The International Jew: The World's Problem." These articles, posted in Ford's newspaper, The Dearborn Independent, propagated risky stereotypes and conspiracy theories, attributing worldwide unrest and financial problems to an alleged Jewish conspiracy. The inflammatory content cloth contemplated Ford's defective beliefs and may come to be a stain on his reputation.

The collection, compiled right right into a e-book titled "The International Jew," become disseminated globally, reaching a huge goal marketplace. Ford's financial backing and endorsement lent credibility to those troubling narratives. The controversial guides not great fueled anti-Semitic sentiments however additionally added on a cascade of results that could reverberate through Ford's private and public existence.

Repercussions on Ford's Public Image

The fallout from Ford's anti-Semitic publications have grow to be rapid and huge. The American Jewish community, appalled with the useful resource of the blatant prejudice propagated in Ford's publications, responded with condemnation and outrage.

Prominent Jewish figures, together with Louis Marshall, openly criticized Ford's perspectives, emphasizing the harmful implications of disseminating such inflammatory content material fabric.

"Whether you watched you may or count on you cannot, you are right." - Henry Ford

In response to the backlash, Ford attempted to distance himself from the debatable articles, claiming that he have been unaware of their content material material material. He issued an apology, disavowing the anti-Semitic narratives and expressing remorse for the harm brought about. However, the damage to Ford's public picture were executed, and the communicate lingered as a darkish shadow over his reputation.

Legal repercussions accompanied as properly. In 1927, Ford issued a proper apology to the Anti-Defamation League (ADL) and distinctive Jewish agencies, publicly renouncing the anti-Semitic content material fabric posted in The Dearborn Independent. As a part of a agreement, Ford agreed to give up the distribution of "The International Jew" and issued a right retraction of the offensive cloth. The prison preference marked a turning aspect, but the scars from the talk endured.

"Obstacles are the ones frightful belongings you notice at the same time as you're taking your eyes off your purpose." - Henry Ford

Despite the efforts to rectify the situation, Ford's affiliation with anti-Semitic sentiments remained a contentious trouble. The controversy resurfaced in 1938 whilst Ford received the Grand Cross of the German Eagle, the very first-class honor bestowed via way of Nazi Germany on non-German residents. The timing, towards the backdrop of developing Nazi anti-Semitism, further fueled complaint and speculation about Ford's ideological leanings.

In the aftermath of World War II and the revelation of the Holocaust's atrocities, Ford's anti-Semitic beyond forged an prolonged shadow. The controversy have turn out to be a long lasting stain on Ford's legacy, prompting reevaluation and condemnation from next generations. The Ford Foundation, established in element as a philanthropic try and mitigate the damage from those controversies, contemplated an acknowledgment of the need for atonement and societal restoration.

As we navigate this tough monetary ruin, it's miles critical to confront the complexities of Ford's legacy. The controversies surrounding his anti-Semitic perspectives and the dissemination of prejudiced cloth underscore the significance of analyzing historic figures of their entirety, acknowledging every their contributions and their flaws. In this nuanced exploration, we grapple with the darker elements of Ford's legacy, spotting that even a pioneering industrialist became not evidence in opposition to the prejudices of his time, and the repercussions of such beliefs should all the time form the narrative of Henry Ford's existence.

Chapter 17: The Great War And Ford's Peace Ship

Ford's Pacifist Stance and the Peace Ship Expedition

In the tumultuous backdrop of World War I, Henry Ford, an industrial corporation rich man or woman of first rate impact, released right into an impressive task that could encapsulate his fervent desire for peace—the Peace Ship Expedition. This financial disaster unravels the intricacies of Ford's pacifist stance during the Great War, exploring the motivations inside the lower back of the Peace Ship, its day ride, and the profound effect it had on Ford's political and public individual.

"If all and sundry is transferring beforehand together, then achievement seems after itself." - Henry Ford

As conflict engulfed Europe in 1914, Henry Ford, renowned for his revolutionary meeting line and automobile upgrades, located himself at a crossroads. A staunch pacifist, Ford's willpower to peace led him to take a powerful step—a transatlantic voyage on the "Oscar II," a supply he chartered for what might become called the Peace Ship Expedition.

Ford's pacifist convictions have been deeply rooted in his perception that wars were now not simplest damaging however furthermore negative to humanity's development. Motivated by a preference to give up the bloodshed, Ford envisioned the Peace Ship as a diplomatic venture that could facilitate negotiations and foster talk a number of the warring countries. His idealistic technique aimed to illustrate that international participants of the circle of relatives and communicate need to be successful over the horrors of struggle.

Impact on Ford's Political and Public Persona

The Peace Ship Expedition, launched in December 1915, carried a severa delegation that protected pacifists, journalists, and fantastic peace advocates. The voyage attracted sizeable interest, no longer simplest for its audacious mission but also for the eclectic combination of human beings on board, representing various ideologies and backgrounds. Ford, on the helm, have grow to be the face of a motion that sought an possibility path to selection in the midst of worldwide battle.

"Failure is in reality the opportunity to begin all over again, this time extra intelligently." - Henry Ford

The day experience faced severa demanding situations from the outset. Ford's idealistic vision collided with the complex geopolitical realities of World War I. His try to mediate peace some of the belligerent worldwide places encountered skepticism, and the Peace Ship have turn out to be a picture of well-intentioned naivety. Despite the genuine efforts to bring about trade, the day ride did no longer advantage its primary goal of influencing the warring international locations to stop hostilities.

The effect of the Peace Ship Expedition extended beyond its diplomatic shortcomings. Ford's foray into global worldwide family members showcased his willingness to use his stature for a purpose large than business enterprise—a departure from the conventional role of industrialists at some point of wartime. However, the excursion's failure brought about a shift in public belief. Ford, as quick as celebrated for his company prowess, confronted criticism and skepticism regarding his functionality to navigate the complexities of world politics.

"You can not assemble a reputation on what you'll do." - Henry Ford

As information of the Peace Ship's pass returned spread, Ford located himself at a crossroads, grappling with the divergence of public opinion. While some famous his willpower to peace, others confused the efficacy of his unconventional diplomatic method. The episode highlighted the demanding situations of translating idealism into tangible diplomatic outcomes and underscored the complexities of navigating the geopolitical panorama.

The Peace Ship Expedition left an indelible mark on Ford's political and public character. It showcased his willingness to challenge the popularity quo and leverage his have an effect on for noble motives. However, the failure of the tour additionally underscored the limitations of person efforts in the face of entrenched geopolitical conflicts. Ford's popularity, as quickly as unassailable, became task to scrutiny, offering a glimpse into the complex interplay amongst business enterprise, politics, and public notion.

"Thinking is the toughest paintings there may be, which is probably the cause why so few interact in it." - Henry Ford

As we delve into this chapter, we navigate the nuances of Ford's pacifist stance and the audacious Peace Ship Expedition. We explore the motivations that propelled Ford to venture past the confines of agency into the world of worldwide global individuals of the circle of relatives. The Peace Ship, a symbol of idealism and ambition, serves as a lens via which we test the complexities of navigating the tumultuous waters of wartime politics and the enduring impact of such endeavors on the legacy of Henry Ford.

Personal Turmoil and Family Dynamics

The Tragedy of Edsel Ford

In the midst of Henry Ford's towering success inside the vehicle enterprise, a poignant financial ruin spread out—one marked via personal turmoil and the tragic future of his most effective son, Edsel Ford. This financial ruin delves into the complexities of familial relationships, the big burden of expectation on Edsel, and the profound effect of his untimely loss of existence on the Ford family dynamics.

"I will construct a automobile for the fantastic multitude." - Henry Ford

Edsel Ford, born in 1893, became destined to inherit the formidable legacy of his father. As the most effective little one of Henry and Clara Ford, Edsel grew up immersed inside the global of cars and agency. From a younger age, he displayed a keen interest in design and aesthetics, a departure from his father's pragmatic and utilitarian technique. Edsel's inventive sensibilities and in advance-questioning vision might later play a pivotal characteristic in shaping the aesthetic evolution of Ford vehicles.

Family Dynamics and the Evolution of the Ford Legacy

The Ford family dynamics had been marked by using way of manner of the interaction of company wishes and personal aspirations. As Henry Ford's imaginative and prescient propelled the Ford Motor Company to remarkable heights, Edsel observed himself navigating the touchy balance between upholding way of life and embracing innovation. Despite his crucial function in the organisation, Edsel faced the daunting task of placing ahead his have an impact on at the same time as strolling beneath the towering shadow of his father.

"Coming together is a starting; retaining together is improvement; working collectively is achievement." - Henry Ford

The dating amongst Henry and Edsel come to be complex, characterised with the beneficial useful resource of a mixture of mutual recognize and divergent perspectives. Henry, an industrial agency titan with a penchant for overall performance, often clashed with Edsel's creative tendencies and choice for layout refinement. This anxiety have become most stated in the improvement of the Model A, in which father and son grappled over format alternatives and production strategies.

The tragedy struck in 1943 at the same time as Edsel Ford succumbed to stomach maximum cancers at the age of 40 9. His untimely demise marked now not great the shortage of a key determine within the Ford

Motor Company but moreover the shattering of a familial pillar. Edsel's death left a void in the Ford legacy, and the demanding situations of navigating succession loomed large.

"Quality way doing it right even as nobody is looking." - Henry Ford

Henry Ford, now in his 80s, confronted the bold venture of making sure the continuity of the own family and organization legacy. The transition of leadership inside the Ford Motor Company end up not without turbulence. Henry's selection to count on a greater active function in enterprise affairs, coupled alongside together together with his reluctance to cede control, introduced stress to the already complicated circle of relatives dynamics.

The submit-Edsel era witnessed the emergence of Henry Ford II, Edsel's son, as a capacity successor. However, the intergenerational struggles that had characterised the relationship among Henry and Edsel strong an prolonged shadow. Henry

Ford II faced the massive undertaking of navigating familial expectancies, corporation responsibilities, and the ever-evolving landscape of the auto agency.

"Whether you observed you can or count on you cannot, you're right." - Henry Ford

The lack of Edsel also brought approximately a shift in the public belief of Henry Ford. The elder Ford, as quickly as celebrated for his enterprise prowess, now confronted scrutiny over his management style and its impact on family dynamics. The tragedy have come to be a turning aspect within the narrative of the Ford circle of relatives, prompting introspection and edition to the converting dynamics in the commercial enterprise employer and the broader cultural panorama.

As we discover this financial ruin, we get to the bottom of the complex tapestry of personal turmoil and circle of relatives dynamics inside the Ford legacy. The tragedy of Edsel Ford's premature loss of life serves as a focal point, illuminating the stressful conditions inherent in the intersection of own family, corporation, and legacy. The evolution of the Ford circle of relatives dynamics could in all likelihood hold to form the narrative of one of the maximum influential car dynasties in history, leaving an indelible mark at the continuing legacy of the Ford Motor Company.

Chapter 18: Legacy In Motion

Assessing Henry Ford's Lasting Impact on Industry

As the pages of Henry Ford's life unfold, we arrive at a juncture wherein the indomitable spirit of innovation and employer meets the inevitability of legacy. This financial disaster delves into the profound and lasting effect that Henry Ford left on the commercial landscape. From the assembly line revolution to the democratization of vehicles, we discover the enduring legacy of someone whose vision transcended his lifetime, shaping the very fabric of modern enterprise.

"Don't discover fault, discover a remedy." - Henry Ford

Henry Ford's legacy is intrinsically tied to the contemporary adjustments he ushered in via the creation of the meeting line. The relentless pursuit of universal performance, coupled with a dedication to affordability, transformed the producing machine. The Model T, with its simplicity, sturdiness, and accessibility, have become a photograph of progress, making car ownership possible for the commonplace American. Ford's innovations no longer most effective redefined the automotive enterprise but set a precedent for manufacturing at some point of severa sectors.

The meeting line, first of all conceptualized for vehicle manufacturing, has grow to be a version for performance and mass manufacturing. Ford's have an impact on extended some distance past his very non-public industry, leaving an indelible mark on production methodologies worldwide. His emphasis on standardization and economies of scale have end up guiding thoughts, streamlining techniques and lowering expenses in sectors starting from electronics to consumer objects.

The Continuing Influence of Ford Motor Company

The Ford Motor Company, based in 1903, emerged as a leading edge of the auto organization below Henry Ford's control. As we decide his legacy, it is not possible to divorce the individual from the organization he constructed. The Ford Motor Company has turn out to be synonymous with American innovation, resilience, and versatility.

"Failure is only the opportunity greater intelligently to start over again." - Henry Ford

Beyond the success of character models, along side the Model T and the Model A, the organisation's willpower to innovation persevered. Ford's introduction of the primary moving meeting line in 1913 became a watershed 2nd that revolutionized not handiest the producing of motors but set a precedent for efficiency in manufacturing worldwide. This groundbreaking method now not nice reduced production time but moreover faded fees, making brilliant devices reachable to a broader client base.

The legacy of the Ford Motor Company extended past production prowess. Henry Ford's vision covered a self-control to employee welfare that became earlier of its time. In 1914, he implemented the five-dollar workday, doubling the triumphing sales for assembly line people. This go with the flow no longer nice multiplied employee delight but additionally have grow to be a catalyst for the burgeoning middle beauty, shaping societal norms and expectations.

"It isn't always the corporation who can pay the wages. Employers first-class address the money. It is the consumer who will pay the wages." - Henry Ford

The Ford Motor Company's self-discipline to innovation continued thru subsequent a long time. From the appearance of the iconic Ford Mustang in 1964 to the improvement of electrical and hybrid vehicles inside the twenty first century, the business enterprise maintained its characteristic at the forefront of the car organisation.

As we navigate the legacy of Henry Ford, we stumble upon a dynamic interaction amongst character genius and institutional continuity.

The Ford Motor Company, guided via the standards instilled with the aid of its founder, evolved with the instances, adapting to changing consumer desires, technological upgrades, and worldwide disturbing conditions.

"Whether you placed you may in any other case you located you can not, you're right." - Henry Ford

In assessing Henry Ford's lasting effect on enterprise, it's far crucial to apprehend not simplest the tangible upgrades but additionally the intangible legacy of a visionary leader. His emphasis on performance, affordability, and human welfare resonates via the annals of enterprise history. The meeting line, as quickly as an in depth idea, is now a cornerstone of modern production. The Ford Motor Company, a testomony to resilience and versatility, keeps to influence the automobile landscape.

As we conclude this financial ruin, we mirror on the enduring legacy of a person who now not simplest shaped an enterprise but left an indelible imprint at the very essence of innovation. The legacy in movement, set in movement thru Henry Ford, transcends the boundaries of time, making sure that his effect reverberates via the corridors of agency, inspiring generations to go back.

Fordism and its Global Legacy

The Spread of Ford's Manufacturing Techniques

As we navigate the annals of commercial history, the term "Fordism" emerges as a beacon illuminating the transformative impact of Henry Ford's production techniques on a international scale. This bankruptcy delves into the complex internet of activities that brought about the dissemination of Ford's progressive manufacturing strategies, all the time converting the landscape of 20th-century industry. From the meeting line's inception to its a long way-reaching have an impact on, we embark on a adventure that transcends borders and resonates via the corridors of world production.

"What's proper approximately America is that despite the fact that we've got a multitude of problems, we've got got splendid potential—mind and belongings—to do some aspect approximately them." - Henry Ford

The genesis of Fordism lies inside the radical reimagining of manufacturing techniques pioneered via Henry Ford. The implementation of the shifting assembly line at the Highland Park Plant in 1913 marked a paradigm shift in commercial enterprise production. The streamlined, green approach no longer only decreased the time required to accumulate an car however additionally drastically reduced production charges.

Ford's strength of will to affordability and mass manufacturing changed into encapsulated inside the Model T, a vehicle that might turn out to be emblematic of the burgeoning automobile company. As the Model T rolled off the assembly line, it symbolized extra than the shipping of a new era—it represented a seismic shift inside the way gadgets had been artificial.

Fordism and its Influence on twentieth-Century Industry

The impact of Ford's manufacturing techniques transcended the confines of the auto industry. The assembly line, a idea to start with conceived to streamline car manufacturing, have turn out to be a blueprint for performance during diverse sectors. The Ford Motor Company, propelled through the fulfillment of the meeting line, emerged as a leading fringe of business innovation, putting precedents that reverberated thru the 20 th century.

"Quality approach doing it right at the same time as no man or woman is asking." - Henry Ford

Fordism's have an effect on extended past america, carrying out at some point of oceans and continents. European industrialists keenly positioned the achievement of Ford's techniques, spotting the capability for transformative change of their personal production landscapes. In the aftermath of World War I, the reconstruction efforts in Europe supplied a fertile ground for the implementation of Fordist standards.

Ford's manufacturing techniques found a receptive goal market in publish-battle Europe, in which the vital to rebuild infrastructure dovetailed with the want for green manufacturing. The adoption of meeting line techniques have become an indicator of enterprise rejuvenation, catalyzing economic restoration and laying the inspiration for the continent's put up-warfare resurgence.

"There is one rule for the industrialist and this is: Make the amazing outstanding of merchandise feasible at the lowest price possible, paying the very best wages feasible."
- Henry Ford

The ideas of Fordism had been no longer restrained to the auto zone. Industries beginning from electronics to textiles embraced the ethos of standardization and mass production. The meeting line, as soon as an avant-garde concept, have turn out to be a ubiquitous function of modern production, reshaping the worldwide economic landscape.

The effect of Fordism on tough artwork dynamics end up in addition profound. The creation of the meeting line necessitated a professional team of workers adept at particular duties, fundamental to the upward push of specialized jobs. While this specialization extra relevant overall performance, it furthermore sparked debates approximately the dehumanizing nature of repetitive, segmented work. Ford, cognizant of the stressful situations, applied the 5-dollar workday in 1914, now not best as a manner of developing wages however also to cope with worries approximately worker pride and retention.

"The simplest actual protection that a person have to have in this international is a reserve of information, enjoy, and capability." - Henry Ford

As we traverse the corridors of Fordism's worldwide legacy, we encounter a complicated interplay of innovation, overall performance, and societal transformation. The meeting line, a symbol of progress, have emerge as every a catalyst for financial boom and a topic of introspection regarding its effect at the personnel.

The Ford Motor Company's affect on global company continued, adapting to evolving technological landscapes and client needs. The mind of Fordism, rooted in ordinary overall performance and affordability, became touchstones for next generations of industrialists, shaping the trajectory of manufacturing well into the 21st century.

www.ingramcontent.com/pod-product-compliance
Lightning Source LLC
Chambersburg PA
CBHW071442080526
44587CB00014B/1954